Map from Classroom Atlas
© 1994 by Rand McNally, R.L. 94-S-175

Sinusoidal Projection
SCALE 1:36,313,000   1 Inch = 565 Statute Miles

Longitude West of Greenwich   Longitude East of Greenwich

0   200   400   600   800   1000 Miles
0   400   800   1200   1600 Kilometers

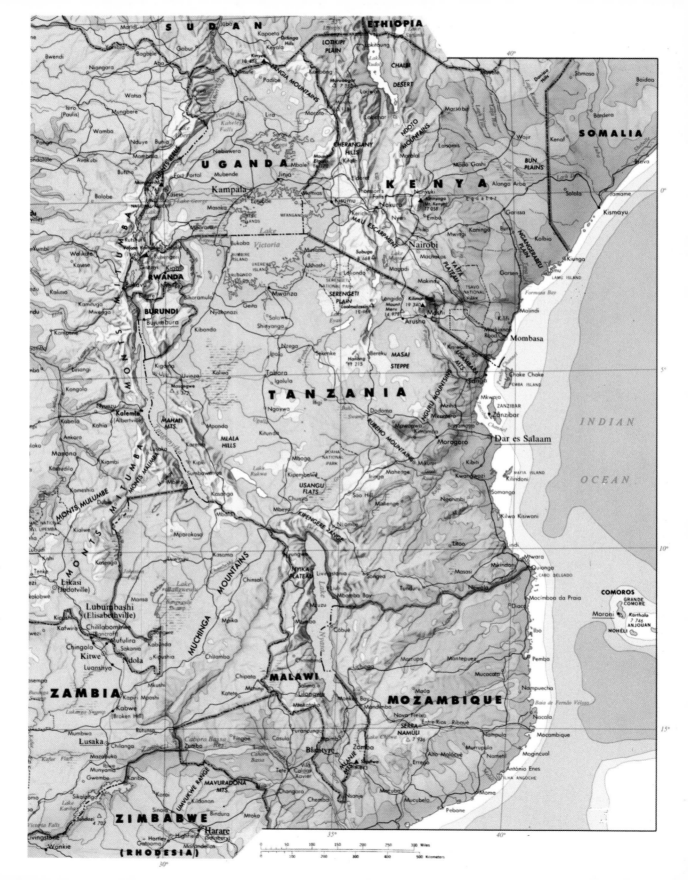

Enchantment of the World

TANZANIA

By Jason Lauré and Ettagale Blauer

Consultant for Tanzania: Richard Lepine, Ph.D., Lecturer, Director, Program of African and Asian Languages, Northwestern University, Evanston, Illinois

Consultant for Reading: Robert L. Hillerich, Ph.D., Professor Emeritus, Bowling Green State University, Bowling Green, Ohio; Consultant, Pinellas County Schools, Florida

CHILDRENS PRESS®

CHICAGO

Millions of wild animals, including gazelles (left) and lions (right), live in Tanzania.

Project Editor: Mary Reidy
Design: Margrit Fiddle

Library of Congress Cataloging-in-Publication Data

Lauré, Jason.
  Tanzania / by Jason Lauré and Ettagale Blauer.
    p.   cm. – (Enchantment of the world)
  Includes index.
  Summary: Discusses the geography, history, government,
people, and culture of this East Africa country.
    ISBN 0-516-02622-4
  1. Tanzania–Juvenile literature. [1. Tanzania.]
I. Blauer II. Title. III. Series.
BT438.B53 1994   93-35495
967.8–dc20   CIP
                                                              AC

Picture Acknowledgments
AP/Wide World Photos: 33 (right), 36 (right), 79, 100
(right), 108 (bottom)
The Bettmann Archive: 21, 28 (2 photos), 29
Bettmann /Hulton: 25 (2 photos), 26, 33 (left)
© **Elk Photo:** © Wezelman, 66 (right)
GeoImagery: © Erwin C. Bud Nielsen, 5, 63
© **Virginia R. Grimes:** 10, 75 (inset), 90 (2 photos)
H. Armstrong Roberts: © S. Holmwood, 4 (left);
© **Frink/Waterhouse,** 10 (inset)

Lauré Communications: © **Jason Lauré,** 11 (left), 17, 19
(top left), 22 (right), 30 (right), 36 (left), 41 (left), 46
(bottom), 48, 52 (2 photos), 55 (2 photos), 57, 58 (2 photos),
61, 64 (right), 66 (left), 67 (3 photos), 68, 69 (2 photos), 71,
72 (top), 74 (2 photos), 75, 77 (left), 81 (2 photos), 82
(inset), 83, 84, 88 (bottom right), 89, 103, 106 (4 photos),
108 (top), 111 (2 photos)
Odyssey/Frerck/Chicago: © **Robert Frerck,** 85, 87, 88 (top);
© **Wendy Stone,** 91 (inset)
Photri: 8, 96 (right)
Photo Agora: © **Robert Maust,** 11 (right), 14, 72 (bottom
left and right), 82, 91, 92 (bottom)
© **Ann Purcell:** 98
R/C Photo Agency: © **Betty Kubis,** Cover Inset, © **Jane H.
Kriete,** 77 (right)
Root Resources: © **Stan Osolinski,** 9
© **Bob & Ira Spring:** 6 (center and bottom right), 102
Tom Stack & Associates: © **Perry Conway,** 92 (top)
Stock Montage: 19 (bottom left and right), 22 (left), 24, 30
(left)
Tony Stone Images: © **Nicholas Parfitt,** 12, 97 (top right);
© **Brian Seed,** 78, 88 (bottom left)
SuperStock International, Inc.: 53, 86; © **Roderick Chen,** 6
(top); © **Horst Cerni,** 50
Travel Stock: © **Buddy Mays,** 94
UPI/Bettmann: 39, 41 (right), 43 (2 photos), 46 (top), 102
(inset)
Valan: © **Stephen J. Krasemann,** Cover, 4 (right), 6 (bottom
left), 64 (left), 96 (left), 97 (left), 100 (left); © **Aubrey Lang,**
15; © **James D. Markou,** 97 (bottom right), 98 (inset)
Len W. Meents: Maps on 89, 91, 102, 105
**Courtesy Flag Research Center, Winchester,
Massachusetts 01890:** Flag on back cover
Cover: Sunrise, Serengeti National Park
Cover Inset: Maasai lady dancer

Young Maasai "warriors" in traditional clothing and jewelry

TABLE OF CONTENTS

A variety of wildlife lives on the vast plains of Serengeti National Park (above); shown here are the crested crane (above right), a leopard (right), and cape buffalo (below).

Chapter 1

A LAND OF CONTRASTS

GEOGRAPHY

Tanzania is a land of vast open spaces, lakes, and millions of animals. It is situated just south of the equator, on the east coast of Africa. Within its 364,900 square miles (945,092 square kilometers) lie the highest and lowest points on the African continent. Its 500-mile (805-kilometer) eastern border is the Indian Ocean. To the north Tanzania shares a long border with Kenya, an invisible line that is no barrier to the animals that migrate back and forth between the two nations.

In the northwest, Lake Victoria forms part of the boundary with the nation of Uganda. The two countries also share a short land border at Tanzania's extreme northwest corner. Along the northwestern border are the smaller nations of Rwanda and Burundi. Moving to the south, a long stretch of the border is marked by Lake Tanganyika; this lake separates Tanzania from the country of Zaire. (Until 1964 Tanzania was called Tanganyika.) Farther south, the border separates Tanzania from Zambia. Tanzania also shares a short section of its border with the nation of Malawi. Lake Malawi forms a portion of the southern border.

A fertile area of Tanzania

The longest stretch of the southern border is formed by the Ruvuma River, which separates Tanzania from Mozambique.

The land is a series of sharply defined highs and lows, many of them created by volcanic upheavals in the past. Tanzania is a dramatic-looking country, varied in climate, topography, rainfall, and wildlife. These differences are reflected in the many different cultures that live here.

HIGH AND LOW POINTS

The great mountain known as Kilimanjaro rises 19,340 feet (5,895 meters). Located just south of the border with Kenya, Kilimanjaro is the highest mountain in Africa. It is also the

Mount Kilimanjaro is always topped with snow.

highest singular mountain in the world, that is, a mountain that is not part of a range. It stands out dramatically from the flat surrounding countryside. Once an active volcano, the now-peaceful mountain is always topped with snow, perhaps the reason why the Maasai called it *Kilimanjaro*, which means "white mountain" in their language. It inspired *The Snows of Kilimanjaro*, a book by Ernest Hemingway. The lowest point in Tanzania—and in Africa—is 2,289 feet (698 meters) below sea level, at the bottom of Lake Tanganyika.

The Great Rift Valley divides Tanzania. The Great Rift is an ancient gash in the earth that runs along the eastern part of Africa from Ethiopia to Mozambique. In Tanzania it shapes the vast plateaus that form much of the center of the country, including the

The Great Rift Valley (above) and a diver exploring coral reefs in the Indian Ocean (inset)

Maasai Steppe. This vast area of open grassland is home to the great herds of wild animals that still roam freely over the land. When traveling in this part of Africa, usually on journeys to see the animals, visitors often have breathtaking views into the rift.

The coast, with its tropical climate and mangrove trees, is home to Tanzania's largest city, Dar es Salaam, the capital. Coral reefs and rich fishing grounds lie offshore. The reefs are part of the islands of Zanzibar and Pemba, which became part of Tanzania in 1964. The islands are made entirely of coral. Mafia Island, also part of Tanzania, is situated south of Dar es Salaam. Other, very small islands also lie off the coast. Many parts of the offshore coral reef are visible.

Lake Manyara (left) in the northeast and a village on the shore of Lake Victoria (right)

LAKES

Tanzania's most famous lake is Victoria, the largest lake in Africa, with a surface covering 26,828 square miles (69,484 square kilometers). Half of the lake is considered part of Tanzania, most of the other half belongs to Uganda, and a small portion in the east is part of Kenya. It is a freshwater lake whose outlets flow to the north, where they are carried along by the Nile until they eventually reach the Mediterranean, more than 4,000 miles (6,437 kilometers) away. Lake Victoria is well known for its fishing and is home to the Nile perch and tilapia. The towns around the lake are served by a variety of boats, including ferries of all shapes and sizes. People also live on the islands in the lake, including Ukerewe, where the Kerewe people live and survive by fishing.

LAKE TANGANYIKA

The long, narrow Lake Tanganyika is an unusual body of water. At 419 miles (674 kilometers) in length, it is the longest freshwater lake in the world, and extremely deep–its waters in some places reach down 4,823 feet (1,470 meters). Because of this great depth,

During the dry season rivers dry up and land becomes parched.

the lake is like an archaeological site, but one that is filled with water. Although the surface of the lake can be rough as an ocean during a storm, the lower levels of the water remain undisturbed and are thought to be millions of years old.

LAKE NYASA

The third of Tanzania's major lakes is Nyasa, also called Lake Malawi. This narrow, deep lake forms part of Tanzania's border with Malawi. About two hundred different species of fish have been found in the lake, and more than three-fourths of them are unique to it.

RIVERS

Tanzania is crisscrossed with an extensive system of rivers. The major rivers are the Ruvuma, marking the southern border with

Mozambique; the Rufiji, which crosses the Selous Game Reserve in the southeast; the Wami, which reaches the coast just opposite Zanzibar Island; and the Pangani, coming from the north and flowing into the Indian Ocean just below Tanga. During the rainy season, these rivers wash the lands with water, especially the Rufiji, whose tributaries collect water from nearly one-quarter of the total area of the country. Many of the smaller rivers are seasonal–they flow only during the rainy season. After the rainy season, some become very shallow, others become little more than marshy land where it is difficult to tell that a river flows through at all. If the flow of the rivers could be controlled, more land would be available for agriculture.

CLIMATE

Temperatures in Tanzania change little throughout the year because of the country's position just south of the equator. At low-lying points such as Dar es Salaam, year-round temperatures average about 90 degrees Fahrenheit (32.2 degrees Celsius). At Arusha, with an elevation of 4,550 feet (1,387 meters), temperatures are between 72 and 85 degrees Fahrenheit (22.2 and 29.4 degrees Celsius). The temperature drops considerably at night in the interior. The biggest weather change occurs during the rainy season, which lasts for several months. The rainy season varies from the north to the south of the country. In the north, it usually rains heavily during part of every day from March through May or June. In the south, the rainy season begins around October or November and continues through March.

Valuable topsoil is lost after the heavy rains.

When the rains come, they are so heavy that bridges and roads are washed out. Topsoil is lost as the water flows to the sea or to local lakes. In most of the country, there is no rainfall at all during the rest of the year. Rainfall varies greatly in different parts of the country. Near Lake Nyasa, there may be more than 100 inches (254 centimeters) of rain a year, whereas in the central plateau less than 20 inches (51 centimeters) falls in an average year.

In some years, the rains do not follow the predictable patterns. When they do come, sometimes they are so heavy that people cannot even leave their homes. Since the great majority of people in Tanzania depend on farming for their livelihood, rainfall is very important to their lives.

San rock paintings

Chapter 2

ANCIENT TIMES: TRADE AND EXPLORATION

ARRIVAL OF THE FIRST PEOPLE

Millions of years ago, the country we call Tanzania was home to the earliest ancestors of humans. It has been populated with people like us for more than ten thousand years. Many of the people who live in Tanzania today are directly descended from those who began to move into the territory about two thousand years ago, but some came as recently as the eighteenth century.

The first modern people were part of the group of hunter gatherers known as San (Bushmen) and Khoikhoi (Hottentots). Evidence of their presence can be seen in rock paintings. The first direct ancestors, sometimes known as Cushites, moved into the northern part of Tanzania from Ethiopia and migrated southward. A little later, groups of people speaking Bantu languages moved into Tanzania from western Africa. They were followed, perhaps a thousand years later, by the ancestors of the Maasai people. The area just to the east of Lake Victoria was inhabited around the year 600 to 400 B.C. Few of these people moved into central Tanzania, however, even in the centuries that followed. In some areas there was not enough rain to sustain them, and other areas were infested with tsetse flies that killed their cattle. Bantu-speakers replaced Cushite settlers here around 200 to 300 A.D.

The coastal region of Tanzania developed separately. The coast was open to exploration from seagoing people and attracted Arabs from the Persian Gulf area as early as the ninth century. By the thirteenth century, the most important town on the coast was the island city of Kilwa Kisiwani. Its position enabled its people to control the sea routes and the transport of gold that was being brought out by Africans from the interior of the continent. It maintained this dominant role until the fifteenth century, when it was surpassed by the island of Zanzibar and the city of Mombasa (now part of Kenya), farther up the coast. The traders in Kilwa and the other coastal cities were Shirazi people who came from the country now called Iran. Their descendants still live on the Tanzanian coast and on Zanzibar, along with the other Bantu-speaking people from the mainland who did not assimilate so many seafarers into their land and culture as the coastal Africans did.

THE FIRST TRADERS

The coastal area of East Africa, including the section that would become Tanzania, was well known to Arab traders from the

These graceful dhows have been in use for centuries.

Persian Gulf, who sailed up and down the coast in graceful sailing ships called *dhows*. It is believed they had clearly established trading routes by about A.D. 100. Taking advantage of the shifting monsoon winds, they were able to travel north and south at different times of the year. The Arabs brought manufactured goods to the people who lived in the region: axes, knives, spears, cloth, and other products. They traded these for the natural products brought by the local people, including ivory, rhino horn, tortoiseshell, timber, and coconut oil. By the ninth century the Arabs began building settlements in the region, which they called the Land of Zanj, which meant the land of the blacks. This is probably how the island of Zanzibar got its name.

Trading posts and small settlements were well established by

17

the twelfth century; from then until the arrival of the Portuguese at the end of the fifteenth century city-states predominated. There were so many Muslims by this time that mosques, the buildings in which they worship, were erected. Where archaeologists find mosques in their excavations, and when they were built, gives them some idea of when the coastal Bantu people began to assimilate the seafarers and adopt their religion as their own. Contact between Arab and Bantu peoples was part of daily life. Much of the settlement was confined to the offshore islands, notably Zanzibar and Pemba, because these were safe from attacks by the mainland people. The mix of culture and language eventually led to creation of a new language, called *Swahili*. Swahili was based on the Bantu language spoken by the local coastal African people (they called their language *Kingozi*). It borrowed much technical and religious vocabulary from Arabic, Persian, and later even Hindi. The widespread use of Swahili throughout East Africa today is a result of this long period of trade and contact, especially trade under the sultans of Zanzibar during the mid to late 1800s. During the European colonial period English (and a little German) became another source of borrowings; at that time, the language was also standardized. Today about fifty million people speak Swahili. The Arabs continued to maintain cultural ties to their homelands in the Persian Gulf and southern Arabia. The impact they had on local life was confined to the coastal regions and the offshore islands.

THE PORTUGUESE

The Portuguese were the next outsiders to arrive in the region. Like the Arabs they were skilled sailors and had enormous impact on coastal regions all over the world. In 1498 the Portuguese explorer and sailor Vasco da Gama arrived in East Africa. He was

The Portuguese, led by Vasco da Gama (above), destroyed the royal castle at Kilwa Kisiwani (left) and erected their own buildings, which are now ruins (above left).

followed by Portuguese forces. The Portuguese were so aggressive that within eight years Portugal controlled the coast and all the trade in the region. They destroyed the city-state of Kilwa Kisiwani, which had been the most important settlement on the coast up to that time.

The balance of power shifted back and forth between the Portuguese and the Muslims, but in the end the Muslims from Oman, a small region on the Arabian peninsula, won. In 1698, exactly two centuries after they arrived, the Portuguese were driven out completely. Unlike the Arabs, whose culture and language were absorbed by the local people, the Portuguese left scarcely a trace of their presence. One of the most significant legacies of their brief control of the region was the introduction of cassava, a root crop that is a basic foodstuff.

Battles back and forth between various powers kept the island of Zanzibar largely free of foreign control until the end of the eighteenth century, when the sultan of Oman established a base of operations at Zanzibar. He soon took control of the island of Pemba as well as significant portions of the East African coast, north to the coastal city of Mombasa in what is now Kenya. The development of Mombasa and the island of Lamu (now part of present-day Kenya) was so similar to that of Zanzibar that even today they clearly can be seen to share a common culture, history, and language.

The fortunes of the people and of the region would soon change dramatically, thanks to the spice called cloves. The discovery that this vital spice, used in preserving and flavoring meat in the days before refrigeration, could be grown successfully on Zanzibar and Pemba brought with it the need for labor–slave labor.

THE SLAVE TRADE

The trade in human beings, known as the slave trade, came about because of the European and Arab desire for laborers. They had a constant need for people to work in their plantations and, of course, they could make the most profit if they didn't have to pay the workers. Only slaves could be made to work under those conditions. By the end of the eighteenth century, Kilwa had reemerged from its destruction by the Portuguese to become an important town on the Indian Ocean trade network. Slaves were brought there to be shipped to French plantations on the Indian Ocean islands of Madagascar, Reunion, and Mauritius. Later, when clove

Men captured by the Arab traders to be sold
as slaves were often starved on the sea voyages.

plantations were established on Zanzibar and Pemba, there was additional demand for slaves in that region.

The mainland town of Bagamoyo also was a place where slaves were brought from the interior before being shipped out, never to see their homelands again. *Bagamoyo* has been translated "to lose hope" or, more literally, "where the heart lays down its burden." Both indicate the despair of the people who were brought there as slaves. The people were wrenched from their homes by the Arab traders who pushed into the interior. By 1840 slaves were being traded at Lake Tanganyika. The slave trade was helped along by the leaders of the people who were being taken. Many of the chiefs were eager for the weapons the traders offered them. Often the slaves had been captured from other groups during warfare.

The European powers as well as the sultan of Zanzibar signed

Humans were sold as slaves in a market in Zanzibar (left) and kept in this cave (right) before being shipped out by boat.

an agreement in 1822 that outlawed slavery, but that treaty only outlawed selling slaves to "Christian" nations. It did not include the Muslim world, which included the Arabs of Zanzibar. The practice of slavery continued until much later in the nineteenth century.

GROWTH OF ZANZIBAR

Although the various Arab clans fought for supremacy in the region, the island of Zanzibar prospered. It grew into the most important trading center in the region. With the help of the British government, it came under the control of Sayyid Said, the sultan of Oman. Although the British had pressed Said to stop sending slaves to Christian markets, he had another important outlet for them—the plantations on Zanzibar and Pemba.

The growing importance of the islands and the coastal towns across from them attracted traders from outside the region— notably Americans. American whaling ships, roaming the oceans of the world in search of whales, would stop at the coastal towns along the East African coast to restock their provisions. After making a treaty with the sultan of Zanzibar in 1833, the Americans established the first consulate at Zanzibar in 1837, even before the British. Both France and the Hanseatic Republics (later to become Germany) made treaties as well. The German presence in the region would grow into political interests before the nineteenth century was over.

THE MISSIONARIES

Closely tied up with the commercial interests of the various nations involved in the region were the explorations by men trying to settle questions of geography, as well as the missionaries who were often hard to distinguish from the adventurer explorers.

The German missionaries Johann Krapf and Johannes Rebmann, representing the British Church Missionary Society, traveled in the region of Mount Kilimanjaro in the late 1840s. They were well ahead of the British explorers Richard Burton and John Speke, who traveled inland from the coast, reaching Lake Tanganyika in 1857. Although its origin is not clear, Tanganyika is thought to come from two words, *Tanga*, which was an important coastal town at this time, and *nyika*, which means "dry earth" or "hinterland," the area just beyond the tropical coast. The Germans combined the two words, saying they were going to Tanga and beyond.

An artist's view of Zanzibar in the nineteenth century

THE EXPLORERS

The island of Zanzibar was the traditional starting point for explorers throughout the nineteenth century. The port of Zanzibar was the best natural harbor for the sailing ships that brought explorers and adventurers from Europe. In Zanzibar they arranged for guides and hired laborers for the harsh overland travel across the territory of Tanganyika.

In 1856 Richard Burton and John Speke intended to explore the vast, unknown regions of central Africa, searching for the source of the Nile. In their day, such an exploration was like sending a man to the moon, but without a spaceship.

They began their journey at Zanzibar, where they arrived on December 20, 1856. Burton expected to be away for at least a year. Can you imagine the amount of supplies he would need, and how many men he would require to carry those supplies as his party made their way into regions that didn't even have trails to follow? It took the men six months to gather all the materials they

John Speke (left) and Richard Burton (right)

needed. Burton, who learned languages very easily, was soon able to speak Swahili. From his book, *Zanzibar: City, Island and Coast*, we learn much about the island during that period, including its role as the shipping point for slaves.

From Zanzibar the explorers and their bearers sailed across the channel that separated the island from the mainland to the town of Bagamoyo, the coastal gathering point for the slaves who had been taken from the interior of the continent.

It took them five months to travel 500 miles (805 kilometers). Sometimes they covered no more than 2 miles (3 kilometers) in a day, at a huge cost of men and donkeys as well as Burton and Speke's own health. They passed through villages that had been destroyed by slave traders. They were attacked by malarial mosquitoes, termites, ants, and tsetse flies.

Yet after a month's rest, they pressed on, picking up their journey again. They had heard of a great lake known as the Sea

A group portrait of the local guides who helped John Speke in his explorations.

of Ujiji. By the time they reached the lake the two explorers were barely able to walk, and Speke was virtually blind. Yet they persisted in exploring this body of water, now called Lake Tanganyika. What drove them to go on, in spite of their life-threatening illnesses? They hoped to answer the question of their century: What body of water was the source of the Nile? At the end of their explorations, they hoped to leave the world a better-known and, therefore, more understandable place. It was Speke who actually first reached a huge lake that he declared to be the source of the Nile. He named it Lake Victoria, after the reigning British queen. But he never made his way around the lake to see if the Nile really did rise from it. The job remained unfinished.

DAVID LIVINGSTONE

Trade and missionary explorations reached their peak in the work of David Livingstone, who went to Africa as a missionary but soon turned his attention to opening trade routes. Livingstone had the idea that increased trade would help end the horrible practice of slavery by giving the people a different way to earn money. But his efforts to blaze trails had exactly the opposite effect. Opening up the routes just allowed the slave traders better access to the interior of the continent.

Livingstone also was obsessed with finding the source of the Nile. In 1866 he set out on a long, difficult expedition. He was not heard from for three years, so people in Europe and in America wondered if he was lost or even dead. Henry Stanley, a newspaperman working for *The New York Herald*, set out on a much publicized search for Livingstone and eventually found him at Ujiji. Although Livingstone was completely out of funds and supplies, he didn't consider himself lost, and was somewhat surprised to be "found."

Though it was now twenty years since Burton and Speke's expedition, traveling through this part of Africa still involved many life-threatening situations. The malaria-carrying mosquito was enough to do in some explorers; there was no treatment for malaria then. (It remains a potentially fatal infection even today.) The terrain itself was treacherous because it was uncharted. Flash floods might sweep through during the rainy season and wipe out whole villages. The bearers hired to carry the expedition's enormous supply of provisions were equally vulnerable to malaria. Such parties were often attacked by groups they

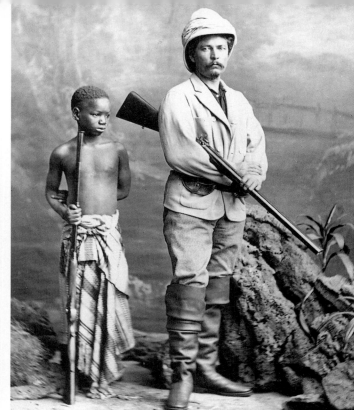

David Livingstone (left) and Henry Stanley (right)

encountered along the way who took their supplies, especially the guns they carried. Chiefs who had power over their own regions often refused permission for the explorers to pass through their territory or allowed them to do so only after taking much of the explorers' goods, often such essential equipment as their compasses, the basic tool of navigation.

Livingstone inspired Stanley to become an explorer. Stanley took up the search for the source of the Nile. Like the others, he began his journey at Zanzibar, setting off on a trip that in its first year reached Lake Victoria. In time, he would sail entirely around Lake Tanganyika and disprove one of Livingstone's theories—that Lake Tanganyika was the source of the Nile. Eventually, Stanley made his way around Lake Victoria and proved that Speke had been right when he said it was the source of the Nile.

German Chancellor Bismarck

Chapter 3

THE COLONIAL ERA

GERMANS ESTABLISH A COLONY

During the end of the nineteenth century European countries laid claim to vast areas of land in Africa. Land was sometimes claimed simply to keep it out of the hands of a rival European power. Such was the case with Tanganyika, where the British and the Germans were trying to keep one another from gaining control.

The Europeans were not interested in all of Tanganyika, only the fertile sections where the farmland and climate suited them. The center of their competition was the land around Mount Kilimanjaro. In 1884-1885 most of the land that the Europeans were fighting over in Africa was portioned out at the Berlin Conference. There, under the leadership of German Chancellor Bismarck, the lines between the new African colonies were drawn and agreed to–without consulting any of the Africans who lived in those regions.

German agent Carl Peters (left); public baths (right)
built by the sultan of Zanzibar

But no one had as yet claimed Tanganyika. Immediately after the conference, Bismarck announced that the land was his. He based his claim on the "treaties" negotiated with local African chiefs by a German agent named Carl Peters.

UNDER GERMAN RULE

The Germans had acted to take control of Tanganyika to protect the interests of German traders in Zanzibar. The British, who had taken control of Kenya just to the north, wanted to maintain good relations with the Germans. British missionaries and traders were working in areas controlled by the Germans. But in pleasing the Germans they angered the sultan of Zanzibar by forcing him to give up his claims to the interior of Tanganyika and to allow safe passage along the coast that he controlled. The sultan was no match for the British, who had superior military and naval strength.

The Germans and British agreed to divide up the sultan's territory. In 1886 they granted him the islands of Zanzibar, Pemba, and Mafia along the Tanganyika coast, and also the island of Lamu. The Germans acquired a fifty-year lease of the coastal lands of Tanganyika from the sultan.

Rule of the territory was granted to the German East Africa Company, but the company's agents were so aggressive the Africans rebelled. In 1891 the German government was forced to take over the administration of the territory, which was considered part of German East Africa. Germany controlled present-day Rwanda and Burundi and a small section of Mozambique. Resistance to German rule soon spread through the territory. The Africans, especially the people known as the Hehe, had been fighting one another for control of the territory and had come to rule a major portion of the land. They soon came into conflict with the Germans and fierce battles followed, with great loss of life on both sides.

During their rule the Germans established plantations for coffee, cotton, and sisal and began work on a railroad to transport the crops to the ports. They forced the Africans to work on the plantations by imposing a tax on their huts that had to be paid in cash.

The last major rebellion against German rule began in 1905. It was known as the *Maji Maji*, "water, water," Rebellion. The people drank a medicine made of water and grain that they believed made them immune to German bullets. The people were led by a medicine man named Kinjeketile, who believed in the power of spirits. The rebellion was widespread and continued until 1907. At least twenty-six thousand Africans were killed.

After the end of the rebellion, the Germans ruled for just seven more years. They began to improve their treatment of the Africans, but most of the concern and care for the people was shown by the missionaries. It was in missionary schools that most people received an education. The missionaries helped to spread the use of Swahili, bringing it to the interior from the coast, as had the traders before them. The people were expected to convert to whatever form of Christianity the missionaries preached, and many of them did. But along with religion, they also were being taught that European ways of living were better than their own.

THE COLONY CHANGES HANDS

When World War I broke out in Europe in 1914, the colonies in Africa became distant battlegrounds for the same warring factions. Tanganyika (and neighboring Kenya to the north) were caught up in this faraway conflict. One of the most important events of the war was the sinking of the German cruiser *Konigsberg* in 1915 where it was hidden in the jungle growth of the Rufiji River. Among the soldiers waging war was Englishman Frederick Selous, known before the war as an elephant hunter. He was killed by a German sniper.

At the time the colonies became involved in the war, in August 1914, there were about 5,300 Europeans in German East Africa and 7,650,000 Africans. The Africans had little choice in becoming part of the war effort. The Germans chose their African soldiers from groups that were accustomed to fighting—but against each other. They had a tremendous advantage in the bush over the European whites, being better able to resist local illnesses and insects and being accustomed to the climate.

From their colony in Kenya, the British began a naval blockade

Frederick Selous (left) was an elephant hunter before World War I. The German troops were led by General Paul von Lettow-Vorbeck (right).

of Tanganyika in August 1914. Then in March 1916, they began pushing into German territory around Kilimanjaro. They didn't have an easy time of it. Although Germany's troops were greatly outnumbered, they were led by General Paul von Lettow-Vorbeck, who is considered a military genius. He introduced the concept of guerrilla warfare into the battle, using knowledge of the land to outwit the British. Although the rest of the region was under the control of the British and their allies, General von Lettow-Vorbeck did not surrender until after the armistice in Europe. The German soldiers were not pushed out of Tanganyika until the end of 1917. The land the British took over had been devastated. During the war it was not possible for the people to grow food. More than 100,000 people—both troops and civilians—are thought to have died during the conflict, from the fighting, the famine, and an influenza epidemic that followed.

THE BRITISH MANDATE

The British ruled Tanganyika informally until 1922, when the newly formed League of Nations officially gave the British responsibility for the region as a "mandated territory." Faced with getting the territory back to a productive state after the devastation of the land and the people, the British decided to institute a policy known as "indirect rule." This meant they would work with the traditional system of chiefs and laws. The British treated the region very much as "their" place, traveling back and forth between Tanganyika and Kenya with little formality. At border towns such as Namanga, travelers signed a book; there were no visas required to cross from one territory to the other.

AFRICAN ASPIRATIONS

As growing numbers of Africans received better educations, they began to develop their own political awareness and the need to protect their rights. The African Association was created in 1929. Many of its members were teachers and civil servants. A similar association that had formed on Zanzibar affiliated with the mainland group in 1939. These groups formed the beginnings of the territory's political structure.

Development of the territory was very slow and made even slower by the worldwide Depression of 1929. When World War II broke out, an estimated eighty thousand Tanganyikans served in the British armed forces, not only in Africa but also in Burma, a country in Asia. During the war the British tried to increase food production in the territory, which had been neglected in favor of cash crops.

BRITISH RULE LOOSENS

At the end of World War II the United Nations was formed. Territories that had been mandates under the old League of Nations were now called "trust territories." This meant that although countries such as Great Britain were directly in charge, these regions had someone else looking after their best interests and that was the United Nations. Great Britain was not happy about this change because it gave the people in the territories a voice in how they were governed; they were given seats on the Trusteeship Council. This was the first time since Europeans first arrived on their continent that Africans had a voice in their own affairs.

Some of the more enlightened officials in the British Colonial Office could see the handwriting on the wall. They could see a day in the future when the territories would be ready for self-government. They wanted to develop local, elected leaders who would be able to take on that responsibility. Their views were dismissed by the governors who continued to rule the territory. Instead, the governors put in place various plans for the territory, ignoring the need for higher education or better technical training. Whatever money was available was used to build a system of roads for transporting agricultural production. This gave the territory an extensive network of roads.

The British Colonial Office had little success in helping the people of Tanganyika become more involved in governing themselves on the local level. The British did not have a good understanding of what the people needed or how village government worked. The Africans began to organize themselves, forming welfare associations. In 1948 the African Associations

Julius Nyerere (left), shown voting in 1958, was the leader of TANU.
In 1962 Nyerere (right) became president of Tanganyika and
said good-bye to the last governor-general Richard Turnbull.

became the Tanganyika African Association (TAA), with more
political purposes. The TAA also fought against racial
discrimination in Tanganyika.

NYERERE EMERGES AS LEADER

The British government strongly disapproved of TAA's growing
influence and acted to prevent any civil servants, including
teachers, from joining any political movement. In 1954 TAA
became the Tanganyika African National Union (TANU), with
Julius Nyerere as its leader. Although educated to be a teacher,
Nyerere soon was forced to resign from teaching, and he began
working full-time for the people's rights. It was clear that the only
way to achieve those rights was to gain independence.

Great Britain tried hard to prevent TANU from gaining ground,
sometimes refusing local branches the right to register as legal
associations. Britain thought it was acting in the best interests of

the Africans, who they believed were not capable of leading themselves. But if Africans were continually denied the chance to gain experience in self-leadership, they would never be ready. The people were forced to take steps to gain control over their own lives, and this was TANU's program, spelled out in 1954: that Tanganyika be prepared for self-government. It also eliminated special privileges for the whites and Asians living in the territory. For TANU Tanganyika had to be seen as an African country. For the British it was a multiracial country with a tiny minority of whites and Asians who, even so, were to be given equal representation in any legislature that was formed.

TANU also wanted to see the territory move forward as a nation, rather than as a collection of small groups of people, each trying to protect its own interests. Tanganyika had so many of these small groups, and TANU knew that it would never be able to act as a unified country if it did not think of itself as one nation. Gradually many chiefs began to see TANU as the best voice for all the people. When Great Britain allowed the election of "unofficial members" to the Legislative Council in 1958 and 1959, TANU was the overwhelming winner.

MOVING TOWARD INDEPENDENCE

Although the British governor of Tanganyika still resisted moves toward independence, the territory continued to move in that direction. By 1960 the importance of the unofficial members grew, and Nyerere emerged as chief minister of the new Council of Ministers. Working with the colonial secretary, Iain MacLeod, Nyerere and Tanganyika swiftly moved to a phase called "internal self-government" on May 15, 1961. Just seven months later, on December 9, 1961, Tanganyika became an independent nation.

Chapter 4

EARLY YEARS OF INDEPENDENCE

ON BECOMING A NATION

The nation of Tanganyika was not very different from the territory of Tanganyika. There were few educated Africans, the civil service was largely directed by whites from Great Britain, and there was little in the way of an economy. The people, however, had waited a long time for this moment and they wanted to see changes. They especially wanted to exercise some control and to take over the best-paying positions in the government. Nyerere, as prime minister of the new nation, was torn. He realized he could not put people into jobs for which they were not suited. He felt that the people needed to be educated—not only in school but also in life. So in 1962 Nyerere resigned his position and set out to become teacher to the whole nation. This was a remarkable thing for a leader to do. He began to develop his basic theme: that in the past, in traditional African villages, people took care of each other and the community took care of them.

While Nyerere roamed the countryside, explaining his ideas to the nation, Rashidi Kawawa took over as prime minister. Kawawa

*Prime Minister
Rashidi Kawawa*

began to replace many of the British officials with Africans, even if they did not have the same qualifications. In 1962 Tanganyika changed its political structure and became a republic, headed by a president. On December 9, 1962, just one year after he left office, Nyerere returned to participate in elections for president and won overwhelmingly. He was ready to remake the country according to his vision, and he had the power to put his ideas into effect.

ZANZIBAR

The relationship between mainland Tanganyika and the island nation of Zanzibar (including the islands of Pemba and Mafia) dated from long before independence. But Zanzibar developed quite differently, mainly because of its long history of contact with people from trading nations of the world. Following the defeat of the Portuguese in the early 1800s, the sultan of Oman controlled much of the East African coast. By 1837 the sultan oversaw both Zanzibar and Pemba, as well as much of the mainland coast. He was most interested in trade and especially with making Zanzibar an important producer of cloves. The sultan forced the local Africans to work on the clove plantations. When he needed more labor, he forced Africans from the mainland to work there as well.

Between Zanzibar and Pemba, the islands grew three-quarters of the world's supply of cloves. Unlike other one-crop countries that have to depend on the world price of their commodity, such as coffee or cocoa, these islands dominated the crop and the economy of Zanzibar was very strong.

The population of Zanzibar at the time of Tanganyika's independence included Arabs and Shirazi, descendants of the earliest settlers who had intermarried with the seafaring explorers and adopted their religion, as well as a few non-coastal Africans who were descendents of slaves. The people were different not only in race but in culture, and often in religion: both the Arabs and the Shirazis were Muslims; the Africans were either Christians or practiced traditional African religions. Political aspirations were growing on Zanzibar just as they had in Tanganyika. The British, who had gained control of Zanzibar in 1890, were faced with another push toward independence, this one bitterly divided by political differences that could often be marked in racial terms between Arab and African. The Shirazi identified with either group, depending on their political power and social standing. The British had always seen Zanzibar as an Arab state, headed by the sultan. They overlooked the antagonisms and differences that existed. The various political parties jockeyed for positions of leadership as Zanzibar moved toward elections in 1963.

Shortly after elections were held independence came, on December 10, 1963. Unlike Tanganyika, however, elections were followed by a violent revolution in which the anti-royalist Shirazi and their non-coastal African allies turned against the Arabs and an unknown number of people–believed to be at least twenty-five hundred–were killed. Many more fled the island, leaving their

The population of Zanzibar (above) includes Arabs, Asians, many coastal Swahili-Shirazi Africans, and some non-coastal Africans descended from slaves brought to the clove plantations. In 1964 the Africans deposed the sultan and installed Abeid Karume (right) as president.

homes and businesses. The newly elected government was overturned, the ruling power of the sultan was eliminated, and rebellious Africans took over the government under Abeid Karume and the Afro-Shirazi political party. The sultan threatened to come back to power and oust Karume, who turned to President Nyerere for military help. Instead, Nyerere offered the Zanzibaris a political union.

UNION OF ZANZIBAR AND TANGANYIKA

Three months later, on April 26, 1964, Zanzibar agreed to join with Tanganyika to form the United Republic of Tanganyika and Zanzibar. The name was changed (six months later) to the United Republic of Tanzania, fashioned from the names of the two nations–tan for Tanganyika and zan for Zanzibar. It was a curious marriage of very different partners. The two unequal parts of this union share nearly equal power: the constitution dictates that if the president is from the mainland, the vice-president must be from Zanzibar, or the other way around.

Even after the union was created Zanzibar continued on its own course of development with its own president. Nyerere hoped to give Zanzibar protection from other, larger countries that could gain influence over it and ultimately pose a threat to mainland Tanzania. For Zanzibar, the merger assured that protection with little cost. Its expenses as a nation were paid by the TANU, while it was able to spend its income on its own development.

EAST AFRICAN COMMUNITY

In 1967 Tanzania and its neighbors, Kenya and Uganda, formed the East African Community. Their idea was to pool their resources and share certain facilities that were too expensive for each country to support on its own. One of the most important elements of their cooperation was the formation of their own airline, East African Airways (EAA).

While the idea was good, the three countries' leaders were in total disagreement about how to manage their resources, and they did not act cooperatively as they had agreed to. The Kenyans were carrying a large share of the debt that had financed the airline. But political upheaval in Uganda put Nyerere in the position of having to cooperate with Idi Amin, a man Nyerere had condemned. In 1971 Idi Amin overthrew Milton Obote, the legitimate president of Uganda. This was just a few years after the creation of the East African Community. Amin was a brutal ruler who killed many of his own people.

In 1977 East African Airways collapsed under the weight of the debt it had piled up. Tanzania responded to this loss by closing its border with Kenya. It kept all the aircraft and ground vehicles that were on its territory, even though they belonged to Kenya. This spelled the end of the East African Community.

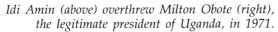

Idi Amin (above) overthrew Milton Obote (right), the legitimate president of Uganda, in 1971.

Tanzania thought that with the border closed Kenya's tourism would suffer and that all the tourists would come directly to Tanzania instead. But just the reverse happened. The tourists had always started their journeys in Nairobi, Kenya, and now they stayed in Kenya.

The loss to Tanzania's economy was tremendous, and it spelled the virtual destruction of its tourist industry. By the time Tanzania reopened its border with Kenya in 1983, it had very little to offer tourists in the way of places to stay, food to eat, or even running water. Things did not really begin to improve until the 1990s. Tanzania's tourism is being redeveloped and is an important part of an economy that has little industry or manufacturing.

Tanzania tried to operate its own airline, Air Tanzania, but it has been unable to keep its small fleet of planes in the air because of maintenance problems. It is known for not keeping to its published schedule.

INVASION OF UGANDA

Even before the breakup of the East African Community, conditions along the Tanzania-Uganda border were very tense.

Having Idi Amin as a neighbor meant that Tanzania's small army constantly had to be on guard. It was impossible to predict what Amin would do next. In 1978 Amin suddenly claimed a piece of territory in the northwest of Tanzania and said it belonged to Uganda. The Ugandan army invaded and occupied this area. Nyerere responded by recapturing the Tanzanian territory, then invading Uganda. He claimed to be doing this on the part of the Ugandans, some of whom were leading the invasion, but most of the soldiers were Tanzanian. The Tanzanian army was increased from thirty thousand men to seventy-five thousand for this battle. They quickly moved through Uganda and reached its capital, Kampala. The cost to Tanzania's economy was tremendous. Money had to be diverted from important projects such as building hydroelectric plants. Food crops had to be supplied to the soldiers, who would ordinarily have been at home growing their own food. Within two years after the successful invasion, the Tanzanian army was down to ten thousand men. Though Nyerere had succeeded in removing Idi Amin, one of the worst leaders Africa has ever known, Tanzania wound up paying the tremendous cost of the invasion.

TAKING CONTROL

In the early 1970s, under Nyerere's rule, Tanzania nationalized many businesses, both large and small. (Nationalization means taking over private property and business and making it part of the government.) The officials of the government thought it was a way to make up for the past, when foreigners had taken over the land. If everything was owned by the government, they thought it would be better for the country and for the people. The idea was to use the money they would make to create a better life for all the people, not just for those who owned the businesses.

When the Tanzanian government nationalized property, teenage members of the TANU political party called Youth Wingers, as well as members of the police and army, would arrive at someone's property and surround it. The property owners would be forced out–often with just the clothes they were wearing and a suitcase. They weren't allowed to take any of their other property, their farm equipment, or their airplanes and motor vehicles. Their bank accounts were seized as well, and suddenly they were left with nothing.

After throwing out the people who were working for their own profit, the government put its own people in their place. But there were very few people who knew how to operate businesses or the large farms that they now controlled. In a few years, most of these businesses and farms stopped producing. For example, there had been a very productive dairy farm near Arusha, a town in Tanzania near the border with Kenya, not far from Mount Kilimanjaro. When the farm was privately owned, it produced so much milk that some of it was sold as far away as Nairobi, in Kenya. But two years after it was nationalized, it was not producing any milk. The people who took it over had slaughtered the dairy cows for their meat and eaten them.

Within half a dozen years, Nyerere's government began asking the same people who had been thrown off their property to come back and start up again. Very few were willing to come back. Many had fled to Kenya, which permitted private ownership of businesses. Now they preferred to remain where they were.

LONG LIVE
MWALIMU
JULIUS NYERERE

ISMAILI JAMAT

*Above: Women of the
Indian community
march in support
of Nyerere. Mwalimu
means "teacher."
Right: Julius Nyerere
is sworn in
as president
of Tanganiyka.*

Chapter 5

THE NEW SOCIETY

NYERERE'S UJAMAA VILLAGES

Tanzania's modern era began after independence. President Julius Nyerere, known to everyone as *Mwalimu*, "the teacher," was determined to find a new system of development for his country. He didn't believe that an economy based on money was suitable for Tanzania. He didn't want to rely on aid or loans from other countries. Nyerere wanted the people to become self-sufficient by growing their own food and providing everything for themselves.

To create this new society, Nyerere declared that everyone would live in a society based on traditional village life, called *ujamaa*. This Swahili word means "familyhood," cooperative life in a big extended family, rather than the urban parents-and-children-only unit with which we are more familiar. President Nyerere wanted everyone to live in some kind of village, not in cities. By 1976 thirteen million people, about 70 percent of the population, were living in 7,684 villages. One result is that even today Tanzania remains one of the least urbanized countries in Africa.

Nyerere believed that this communal living, sharing material goods to make everyone equal, was natural for people in Africa.

Some supporters of the Arusha Declaration of 1967

Acting much as the teacher he was before he became president, Nyerere took on the whole country as his classroom, teaching it how to live in this new/old way. He made his plans known formally in the Arusha Declaration of 1967.

PROBLEMS WITH UJAMAA

Ujamaa proved to be a difficult concept to carry out. It is true that many African people *do* live by cooperating and sharing. But they do so in small kinship groups, with people they are related to, or in small communities. They often are suspicious of people living outside their own circle. They resisted moving from their traditional lands, where their ancestors were buried.

Many people simply refused to move and were forced to by the government. Some people were put in jail. In some instances, people would move to the new area, then slip back to their old homes. So, instead of improving living conditions and agricultural production, the country was producing less food than before.

In traditional Tanzanian cultures, as in virtually all African cultures, wisdom and decision making belonged to the elders. Even during the colonial period, the traditional chiefs and village headmen were part of the process of carrying out colonial policy. In its eagerness to get the ujamaa system working, the government sent out young men, some educated, some not, with no family ties to the headmen, to carry out the policy. There was so much resistance that the government was forced to bring the traditional leaders into the decision-making committees.

NYERERE EXPLAINS HIS VISION

When Nyerere visited one ujamaa village called Shamba Letu, he explained, "You can't eat money; it's nothing but a piece of paper. But what if you made what you were going to buy, instead of using this piece of paper to buy it? We have to worry about producing the things that money was invented for in the first place. If we produce goods the money will follow."

FOREIGN AID

Along with the idea of the ujamaa village, Nyerere stressed the need for *kujitegemea*, "self-reliance." Nyerere believed strongly in the idea of achieving self-sufficiency, because he didn't want Tanzanians to have to rely on aid from other countries, even though Tanzania was one of the biggest recipients of aid in Africa. An important slogan of TANU was *Uhuru na Kazi*, "Freedom and Work." Nyerere wanted the people to understand that they would have to work to truly have the freedom that had come with independence.

Women pound grain to make flour.

WOMEN'S ROLES

Nyerere worked to change the structure of Tanzanian society, including the traditional roles of men and women. Women do a much greater portion of the work in Africa than men. In addition to raising children, most women also grow and prepare the food. This is a time-consuming task. Food is often prepared by pounding grain to make flour, then preparing a meal from the flour. Everything is done without electricity or machinery of any kind. A woman must go out and search for firewood, then carry it back to her home. She must go out each day to get water and carry it back in a bucket on her head. Girls begin carrying small buckets of water when they are very young.

Under Nyerere's direction, a new marriage law was put into place that overruled customary African laws as well as Islamic laws. (It was not put into effect in Zanzibar.) The law gives women certain rights. The minimum age at which women can marry is fifteen, which means girls stay in school a bit longer. Women have more of a say in disputes with their husbands, and in the case of those who follow the Muslim religion, the religion of Islam, a man's first wife has to approve her husband's desire to take a second wife. Muslims believe that a man can have up to four wives at one time, as long as he treats them equally and is able to provide for them.

A NEW ROLE FOR EDUCATION

What Nyerere tried to do for the people of Tanzania was to completely change the way they thought, the way they viewed themselves, and the way they lived their daily lives. One of the most far-reaching plans he had to accomplish this was to alter children's education. He saw education as a way of giving students "a sense of commitment to the total community." He wanted students to have a new set of values, not those they inherited from their former colonial masters. And recognizing that only a small number of students actually move on to secondary education, he wanted primary education to be seen as a complete education, not just a step along the way. Under colonial rule and in most modern African countries since independence, most students don't complete secondary school and see themselves as having failed. Nyerere thought it was better to set a realistic goal that students could achieve. He wanted education to prepare the people for the kind of agricultural life they were likely to live.

About 20 percent of the government's entire budget has been directed toward education. Tanzania, like most African countries after independence, found itself with few skilled, highly educated

*The government not only educates children (left), but
it also has classes for illiterate adults (right).*

citizens, huge numbers of illiterate adults, and millions of children
who needed schools to attend. The whole country had only one
hundred university graduates; all of them had had to go outside
the country to earn their degrees. Tanzania needed every kind of
trained professional–doctors, technicians, engineers, nurses,
business managers–all at once. It tried to do it all, and achieved
certain levels of education. By the late 1970s it is believed that
nearly all seven-year-old children were starting school, a
tremendous change from the time of independence. The number
of children who move on to secondary school has increased
dramatically too, although three-fourths of them are boys. At the
same time millions of adults have learned to read, write, and do
some arithmetic. Today, Tanzania has one of the highest rates of
literacy in Africa. Because it needs so many new teachers,
Tanzania has turned to the United States for Peace Corps
volunteers. There are about one hundred Peace Corps workers in

*An aerial view
of the University
of Dar es Salaam*

the country, most of them teaching math and science at the
highest levels of secondary education. The Tanzanian government
has requested hundreds more.

Tanzania also has two universities, the University of Dar es
Salaam, established in 1961, and Sokoine University of
Agriculture, which opened in 1984.

When it began its educational programs, Tanzania had a student
body that came from 120 different cultures, with as many different
languages. The use of Swahili, however, was already in place
throughout the country, as it was, to a lesser extent, in Kenya. In
all, about fifty million people throughout East and Central Africa
used Swahili as their common language. Therefore, Swahili was
introduced in schools as soon as children and adults started their
education. Having one common language meant that textbooks
could be developed that would be used throughout the country.
English, used widely in business and government, is taught as a
second language.

SWAHILI

The widespread use of Swahili had its beginnings as far back as the ninth century. Swahili is one of the more than four hundred Bantu languages that are spoken by 150 million people today over the entire southern third of Africa. Swahili borrowed vocabulary from Arabic and other languages as a result of trade contact. These borrowings have been traced to the period after the Portuguese decline, the end of the seventeenth century. Modern Swahili began on the coast. Then, like everything else, its use traveled inland with the traders, primarily during the nineteenth century. The name comes from *sawahil*, the Arabic word for coast.

While they ruled Tanganyika the Germans, and later the British, promoted the use of Swahili by government officials and thus set the scene for its adoption by the entire country, as well as by neighboring Kenya. Because it was a language that developed in Africa, it was appealing. Unlike virtually all other countries in Africa, Tanzania did not adopt a colonial or European language as its official language. This helped the people come together as an African nation. Of course, the use of Swahili also was made possible because in Tanzania no ethnic group was large enough to impose its culture on the others. Although all the ethnic groups do have their own languages, which they use at home, as soon as they come into contact with any official, a teacher, the army, or any other institution, they are exposed to Swahili.

Newspapers are published in Swahili and English, and radio stations broadcast in Swahili and English. Local television programs use Swahili (there is television on Zanzibar only). Although not everyone speaks Swahili, it is a valuable tool in the effort to build a united nation from more than 120 different cultures.

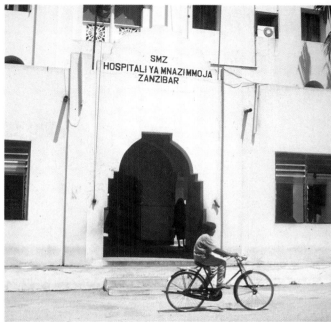

A sign on the beach in Zanzibar, asking people to keep the city clean, (left) is in Swahili. A hospital (right)

HEALTH

The most pressing health problems in Tanzania are diseases carried by insects and parasites. These diseases are basically the same ones that plagued the European explorers more than one hundred years ago. Despite tremendous efforts to bring basic health services to most of the people, the biggest threat to Tanzanians today is malaria, a disease carried by a mosquito that thrives in damp, low-lying areas. These are the same areas that are best for farming, so the people don't have a choice about moving to a better climate. There is no way to prevent malaria, which is often fatal, especially in children. Most children and young adults develop immunity to the disease, although they will continue to suffer attacks. The second most serious disease is bilharzia, carried by water infested with diseased snails.

Sleeping sickness, carried by tsetse flies, also occurs near rivers and lakes. More than two-thirds of the territory of Tanzania is infested with these flies. There has been some success in combating this disease when the bush has been cleared and then treated with insecticides.

Tuberculosis, pneumonia, polio, and common childhood diseases also take their toll. Now AIDS has been added to the list of diseases that affect the population. More than 10 percent of the people living in and around the cities are thought to be infected with the AIDS virus. As in other African countries, AIDS is mainly spread by heterosexual contacts, and to some extent by contaminated blood supplies; infected needles from drug use and homosexual contact are less a factor than they are in developed countries. Because Tanzania is largely rural, it requires its graduate physicians to spend time serving people in the countryside. A plan is in effect to train other kinds of medical workers including medical assistants, rural medical aides, and maternal and health aides.

Many of Tanzania's health issues are made worse by the rapid population growth, estimated to be about twenty-six million. Although Nyerere stressed having fewer children who could be better cared for and established a Family Planning Association in 1969, the high birthrate of 3.7 remains a serious problem.

FLYING DOCTORS

In 1957 a young British physician, Dr. Michael Wood, who was working in Tanzania, saw the need to reach people in the outlying regions of the countryside. People who had health emergencies and needed surgery quickly often could not be reached in time. Because of the great distances and the few physicians available,

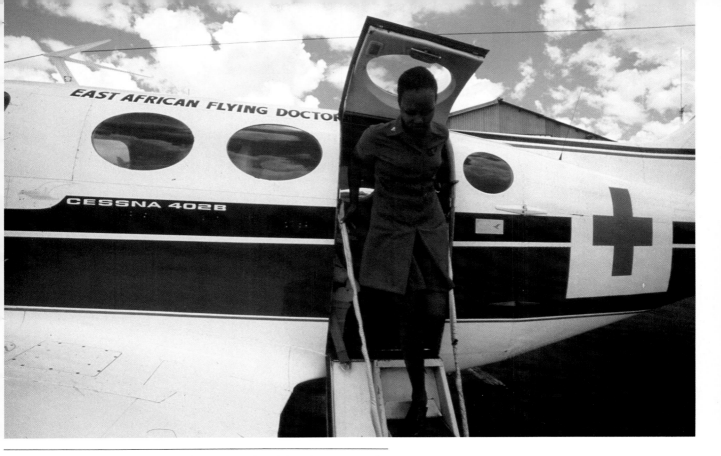

A plane belonging to the Flying Doctors service

many people were without this help. With two other physicians, Wood set up the African Medical and Research Foundation (AMREF), better known as The Flying Doctors. From his base on the slopes of Mount Kilimanjaro, he flew to Arusha each week to treat as many patients as possible.

A system of radiophones allowed the doctors to be informed of an emergency and respond to it by sending out a surgeon. The service began with just one small plane, a Piper Tripacer. Today, it has grown into an important medical institution. In addition to its emergency services, AMREF also offers training for community health workers and does medical research into diseases that affect so many people in East Africa. The Flying Doctors is supported by funds from aid agencies and individuals.

Most Tanzanians live in small villages. Their huts are built with available materials. Roofs are thatch (above) or corrugated tin (below). A village market (below) sells cassava, sweet potatoes, and coconuts.

Chapter 6

A NATION OF
MANY CULTURES

The people of Tanzania, who live mainly in small villages, come from more than 120 different ethnic groups, each with its own history, culture, and language. Although no one group, or tribe, is very large, half the population comes from about a dozen groups. The largest group, the Sukuma, make up 13 percent of the population. None of the rest equals more than 5 percent of the people.

Nearly all of the people–95 percent–are of Bantu origin, a word that refers to their language group. These people, who have certain features in common, probably moved into Tanzania from areas in West Africa beginning about three thousand years ago. The people who moved in from North Africa are of two origins, the Cushitic people from the region of Ethiopia and the Nilotic people from the region of the Nile River. They are different in appearance and in culture from the Bantu speakers, and although small in numbers, they are among the best-known groups in East Africa.

WHAT IS A NATION?

If we were to look at a map of Tanzania drawn according to its ethnic divisions, we would see many tiny territories. This makes it easier to understand why the concept of a "nation" is a relatively new one to most people living in Africa. Even today, most people in Tanzania still live in the same regions as their ancestors did. Kinship is the basis for the community in which groups live. Some kinship links may be quite distant, but the relationship can be traced, usually through oral history. There is a person in each kinship group who can recite this history and who teaches it to someone in the younger generation, who then passes it on. The "family" refers not only to parents and children but also to grandparents, cousins, aunts and uncles, and in-laws. We call this an extended family.

FITTING INTO THE COMMUNITY

In many Tanzanian societies, the individual is seen as part of the group. He or she marries someone who will fit into the group and who will be accepted by the group. Family members may be the most concerned in seeing that a child marries someone suitable, but the community or neighborhood group also is involved in the decision. This is important in an area where neighbors work together to cultivate the land and build houses.

In most Tanzanian societies, descent is traced through the father's line. When a girl is to be married, the family of the boy must pay a bride-price. This helps ensure that the girl will be well treated. The investment is often high and may be paid over a number of years. The family of the boy is responsible for

A family outing at Oyster Bay Beach in Dar es Salaam

providing cattle, if they are a traditional family, or for helping with cash payments if they are in the cash economy. Then the boy's family has a share in the investment. This helps maintain stability within the community. Sometimes part of the marriage payment is made only after the first child is born—or the first son. There is a great emphasis in African families on having children, especially boys.

SUKUMA

Sukuma means "people to the north." Today the Sukuma live around Mwanza, on the southern rim of Lake Victoria, one of the richest agricultural regions in the country. They are well known for performing the *gobogobo* dance and are traditional snake charmers. The dancer wraps a large snake around his body, and dances to the beat of a drum. In Swahili the word *ngoma* means "a drum" and it also means "a dance." Drums often accompany the dances.

CHAGA

The Chaga live mostly on the southern slope of Mount Kilimanjaro, a fertile region with good rainfall. Because the Chaga have always lived at high elevations, they have enjoyed some of the most healthful conditions in the entire country, free from many of the insects and insect-borne diseases that afflict other regions. The Chaga and the Haya were among the people most influenced by Christian missionaries and by Western education. As a result, they hold many positions in the government and are most likely to be found working in the cash economy.

MAASAI

The Maasai are Nilotic people who are distinctive in appearance and in culture. (Maasai is sometimes spelled Masai, but the correct term is Maasai, reflecting the language name, Maa.) The Maasai live in the northern part of Tanzania, along the Kenya border; they also live in Kenya. The Maasai was one of the ethnic groups that was separated when the borders were drawn. The Maasai were such fearsome warriors that their territory remained largely unexplored until the 1870s. The Maasai believe that their god gave them all the cattle in the world. Traditionally, men went raiding to bring back "their" cattle. The Maasai live on a unique diet of blood and milk, which they get from their cattle. On rare occasions, they slaughter and roast a cow for a celebration.

The Tanzania Maasai have much less contact with outsiders than the Maasai in Kenya. But both groups maintain their unique culture. The most notable feature of their way of life is the creation of age sets. An age set is a group of boys who pass

An age set of young Maasai

through ceremonies together. They are usually between twelve and twenty years of age and are recognized by their elders as "warriors," the traditional Maasai term for young men. They have specific responsibilities and rights and remain part of their age set for their entire lives. The Maasai do not have chiefs; every adult male participates in decision making. Every decision is arrived at eventually by agreement among all members.

The Maasai who live around Arusha are called the "agricultural Maasai." They cultivate crops, unlike the "pastoral Maasai," who depend entirely on their cattle and other animals. The Maasai have always lived in harmony with wildlife. Although they keep cattle, like many other groups, they rarely eat meat, and so have never hunted animals for food. Where there are Maasai, the wildlife continues to flourish, as in the Serengeti. In 1959 in recognition of the Maasai's unique relationship with wildlife, a

The Maasai are recognized by their distinctive beaded jewelry.

portion of the eastern Serengeti was returned to the Maasai and became part of their land.

MAASAI CULTURE AND ORNAMENTATION

When they are dressed traditionally, the Maasai are easily recognized by their beaded jewelry, worn by both men and women. The jewelry is made of tiny imported glass beads, in bright colors, that are arranged in patterns. The shapes of the jewelry often tell something about the person wearing it: a woman wears a certain kind of necklace when she gets married, for example. The women make the jewelry for themselves and for the men. In the past they also decorated many objects with beads and used beads on their leather garments.

The influence of the missionaries has resulted in a transitional way of life for some Maasai. When they go to the cities, they wear Western clothing and speak English or other European languages; when they return to the land, they wear traditional Maasai clothing and jewelry and speak their own language. Many people think the Maasai way of life is as endangered as some animal species, but the Maasai have managed to live according to their traditions longer than most ethnic groups.

One of the best-known Maasai in Tanzania was former prime minister Edward Moringe Sokoine. Sokoine University, the agricultural university, was named in his honor.

SCULPTURE

The best-known sculpture from Tanzania is made by the Makonde. They take logs of ebony, a very hard, black wood, and carve several types of sculptures. One kind is a complicated "family tree" statue, which can be as tall as 6 feet (1.8 meters), with figures of an ancestor or ancestors at the top and those of their descendants below them, seeming to climb or make a "human pyramid." It is believed that the Makonde have been making sculptures for hundreds of years.

The Makonde live on the Makonde Plateau in the southeast, next to Mozambique, where they also are well represented. Because of their geographic isolation, the Makonde were not influenced very much by the colonial period. Except for a group that migrated to Dar es Salaam and formed a sculptors' cooperative, they have remained nearly out of reach of the changes taking place in the country since independence. Their territory is still almost impassable, with jungles, rough terrain, and

*A Makonde working on a carving (above);
a carver displays a finished sculpture (right)*

few roads. The Makonde trace their ancestors through the mother's family. Much of the Makonde sculpture is sold in neighboring Kenya, where there are many visitors.

EXOTIC WOOD

While the Makonde carvers are known for their ebony sculptures, there is another wood in Tanzania, *nyinga*, that is prized by musicians. It is the best wood for clarinets, because of the tone that is produced. The best of these, the Buffet clarinets, are made in Paris, France, from nyinga that has aged for many years. Now, because local carvers are using the same wood for their work, the wood isn't allowed to age as long, and newer clarinets have a tendency to crack. But nyinga is still the wood of choice for musicians all over the world.

The artisans of Zanzibar are well known for their wooden

Tinga Tinga painting is done on pottery (left) and on fabric (top). An elegant Zanzibar chest (above)

chests. These trunk-size chests are decorated with metal strips and brass studs arranged in geometric patterns.

A new craft, called Tinga Tinga, is named for the man who created this unique style of painting on wood and other materials. Tinga Tinga's work is colorful and lively, full of dancing figures and village scenes. He taught the style to members of his family and then to more and more people. Today, there is a whole village of people who paint Tinga Tinga in the same style.

India Street in the Asian section of Dar es Salaam

ASIANS

In Tanzania people from present-day India and Pakistan are usually referred to as Asians. They have been the traders and shopkeepers of Tanzania as far back as the period of German colonization. Visitors to Tanzania are often surprised to see Asians running nearly all the small businesses. The Asians usually operate as closely knit family groups, keeping long hours and staying apart from the culture of the country. This is true throughout East Africa, where Asians have been the faces behind the cash registers for generations. Even after they were thrown off their property and had their businesses taken from them during the rush to nationalization, many Asians returned as soon as they were invited back. For many, Tanzania is the only home they know. In Dar es Salaam, Asians are concentrated around India Street, the Asian quarter of the city.

The Anglican Cathedral Church of Christ in Zanzibar (left) is constructed over a former slave market. Muslims celebrating Mohammad's birthday (right)

RELIGION

The population of Zanzibar is a complicated mixture of races. Because it has been on the trade routes of travelers from the Arab and Asian worlds, it has people who can be identified as Arab, Indian, and Bantu, as well as combinations of these peoples. The people are bound together by their common religious beliefs. Nearly all the people of Zanzibar are Muslims. Most of the people on the mainland either are Christians or follow traditional African beliefs. The largest group of Muslims on the mainland are those who live along the coast and are part of the Swahili culture of the islands. Between one-fourth and one-third of Tanzania's total population is Muslim.

The widespread practice of Christianity in Tanzania may be traced to the missionaries who arrived in the mid-1800s. Their emphasis on education was very strong. Johann Krapf, a German working for the English Church Missionary Society, translated the New Testament into Swahili. For many people, this was the only book they could read.

Although one-third of Tanzanians are said to be Christians, many continue to practice traditional religions at the same time. The people often take the parts of the different religions that make sense to them and combine them in a way that works for them. Some African Christians have more than one wife because that works better in their society than the Christian way. When Pope John Paul II attended the Forty-third Eucharistic Conference in Kenya in 1985, Tanzanian bishops traveled there to hear him speak about family planning. He urged the people gathered there not to have more than one wife.

THE PRACTICE OF ISLAM

Muslims, people who practice the Islamic faith, are required to follow the "five pillars" of their religion. They must declare their faith, saying "There is no God but God (Allah), and Muhammad is his Prophet." Muslims must pray five times a day, kneeling on the ground and bending down until their heads touch the earth. They face Mecca in Saudi Arabia when they pray.

Ramadan, the ninth month of the Muslim calendar, is the holiest time of the year. Muslims must fast from sunup to sundown during this month. Muslims must also give alms to the poor and if they can afford it, they should make a *hajj*, or pilgrimage, to Mecca for prayer at least once in a lifetime.

Tanzanian treats for sale at an open-air market include filled pastries and potato cakes.

FOOD

Most of the foods eaten in Tanzania are typical of those found throughout East Africa. The basic food is *ugali*, made from the local grain flour, usually maize (corn). After pounding the maize kernels into a flour, it is cooked into a stiff porridge. Ugali is eaten alone or with meat or fish stew when available. Maize forms not only the basic foodstuff but a large proportion of the entire diet. A local banana dish, *ndizi*, is made from green bananas that have been cooked with meat. The influence of Arabic cooking is found in *pilau* or *biriani*, spicy rice and meat dishes that are the basic food in Zanzibar and along the coast. The kinds of spices used vary with the meat being eaten or the sauce being prepared.

Most Tanzanians have very little meat or fresh vegetables in their diet. Along with maize, people also may grow eggplants and pumpkins. Meat usually is eaten only on special occasions–the birth of a child, a circumcision, or a wedding. Many people roast a young goat, called *mbuzi*, on such occasions.

A variety of crops are grown in Tanzania. A man (above) tends
his vegetable garden. Harvesting beans (below left) and hoeing
a field of maize (below right)

Chapter 7

BUSINESS AND INDUSTRY

THE ECONOMY AND AGRICULTURE

Tanzania's economy revolves almost entirely around agriculture. The industries that exist are largely those owned and operated by government agencies, although there is a continuing movement to turn these over to the private sector.

A variety of food and cash crops are grown in Tanzania. Food crops are grown for the people's own use; "cash" crops are grown for sale. Cash crops include cotton, coffee, tobacco, and cashew nuts. The basic food crops are maize, cassava, beans, millet, and bananas. All of these crops can be grown on the small plots that most people work. When people grow a surplus of these basic foods, they can sell it locally. Sugar, wheat, and rice are grown on large plantations, many of which are still government owned. These crops are meant to be sold outside the country, but that requires a well-planned program with good storage and transportation facilities to get the crops to the marketplace.

Picking coffee (above) on a small farm; the beans are ripe when they turn red (inset).

Coffee is grown mainly on small farms at the higher elevations. It grows well on the slopes of Mount Kilimanjaro and Mount Meru, on the highlands of the south, and along the shores of Lake Victoria. Cotton is grown on small farms in the region south of Lake Victoria. Both cotton and coffee are grown for export.

A SPICE CALLED CLOVE

At one time, cloves were the biggest agricultural success story of Tanzania. They have been grown in Zanzibar, and especially on Pemba Island, for many years. For much of that time, Pemba was the world's leading producer of cloves. This little island, just off Tanzania's coast opposite the port of Tanga, is very fertile, and has just the right growing conditions for cloves. The name *Pemba* means "green island" in Arabic. They have been grown on Zanzibar for about two hundred years, but only after the seeds

A clove tree (above) is surrounded by palms. The flower of the clove tree (inset)

were smuggled there by French traders. Before that, the Spice
Islands of Indonesia had a monopoly on the crop. The clove is an
important spice with many uses. The buds, which grow on trees,
are picked by hand twice a year and then dried in the sun. These
tiny buds are used in flavoring and preserving food. The oil is
also valuable and has many uses. Cloves supported much of
Zanzibar's economy for many years. The island nation grew quite
rich as a result. Recently, however, the Indonesians have come
back into the market. Using cheap labor and planting large areas
with the crop, they have reduced the price paid for cloves
drastically. This has reduced the importance of cloves in
Zanzibar's economy, although nothing has as yet replaced it. It is
not easy to change a country's dependence on one crop. In the
1960s, the islands grew about 20,000 tons (18,144,000 kilograms) a
year. Now they are down to about 8,000 tons (7,257,600 kilograms)
a year.

SISAL

Another crop that used to be important for Tanzania was sisal, a natural fiber used for ropes and carpet backing. Before independence, huge plantations of sisal employed more than 100,000 laborers.

Although sisal was once the most important agricultural export crop for Tanzania, production plummeted beginning in the 1960s. Poor management, lack of equipment, and lack of money to buy spare parts for the equipment sisal farmers did have played a role in this drop. But Tanzania also was hit by a drop in the world price of sisal. Sisal has been pushed aside by synthetic substitutes that are cheaper, lighter in weight, and less likely to rot when exposed to water. The market price for a crop can change quite literally overnight.

DECLINE IN PRODUCTION

As a result of the experiment with ujamaa villages, Tanzania's production of crops, especially those intended to earn foreign exchange, dropped drastically over a ten-year period. The government's control over all phases of production led to inefficient, often corrupt, practices. Storage facilities were, and remain, a serious problem. Even when people have successfully grown and harvested a crop, 30 to 40 percent of it is lost after the harvest because of insect and other damage.

People felt little incentive to work hard because prices were controlled; their efforts rarely resulted in improvements in their lives. Instead, the people put most of their energy into producing food for their families. Since the move back to a market economy,

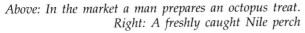

Above: In the market a man prepares an octopus treat.
Right: A freshly caught Nile perch

food production has recovered somewhat. However, it is difficult to keep up with the growing population. Only 5.5 percent of all of Tanzania's vast land area is suitable for farming on a regular basis. Most of that land, 90 percent of it, is worked in small plots by people who have stayed in the ujamaa villages.

FISHING

Three important lakes—Victoria, Tanganyika, and Nyasa—and the warm waters of the Indian Ocean offer rich grounds for fishing. About 60,000 people work full-time as fishermen and more than 300,000 others are involved in fishing and related activities on a part-time basis.

Fishermen who fish the lakes can catch sardines, Nile perch, and tilapia. Both Nile perch and tilapia are delicious African species. Commercial fisheries have been established on the major lakes as well as at the country's dams and along the ocean front.

Customers examine the fresh catch of the day at a restaurant overlooking the harbor.

Tanzania exports part of its catch, including more than a million tons of prawns. However, most of the fish are consumed locally, especially in Dar es Salaam. The need for dependable refrigeration makes it difficult to market fish outside the local area. Much of the catch that is not eaten immediately is dried or smoked so that it will last until it reaches the markets.

Although there are many independent fishermen, most big fishing boats are still owned and operated by the government. When these big boats go out into the Indian Ocean, they often find boats of foreign nations fishing in their territorial waters. There is little they can do. Tanzania wants to negotiate an exclusive economic zone that would extend for 200 miles (322 kilometers) from its shore and make it illegal for foreign nations' ships to exploit Tanzania's fishing grounds.

*Dr. John T. Williamson,
the founder of the
Mwadui diamond mine*

DIAMONDS

Africa is often associated with diamonds, and Tanzania has its
share. Although the best days of its diamond mining are in the
past, the main diamond mine, discovered in 1939, is still an
important source of income. The mine, known as Mwadui for its
location, is also called the Williamson mine, after the man who
discovered it, Dr. John T. Williamson, a Canadian geologist. The
mine produced steadily through the years, reaching its highest
production in 1966 when 924,000 carats of diamonds were
recovered. (An average engagement ring has a diamond that is
about one-quarter of a carat.) After Tanzania's independence the
Tanzanian government and the huge diamond firm of De
Beers/Centenary, through its subsidiary Willcroft Co. Ltd., shared
the mine's ownership. When Nyerere nationalized all the diamond
mines in Tanzania, they were run by the State Mining
Corporation. Diamond mining is a very specialized business, and
after nationalization diamond production fell drastically, from

nearly 1,000,000 carats to 250,000 carats over a period of ten years. By 1989, production was down to 76,000 carats.

In Tanzania, individuals called artisan miners work various sites where diamonds occur close to the surface. They use very simple equipment, and if they're lucky, they can earn a living from their efforts.

GEMSTONE MINING

Diamonds aren't the only precious gems found in Tanzania. There are many small pockets of colored gemstones, some of them near the city of Tanga. One stone–tanzanite–is named for the country. It is a beautiful purple-blue, clear gem that often occurs in large sizes. The color is achieved by "cooking" the stones on a little stove called a *jiko* in Swahili. This brings out the deepest purple-blue color.

Tanzanite is usually mined by individuals working on their own. At times there have been as many as fifteen thousand people digging away in Tanzania, hoping to find tanzanite or other precious colored gemstones. Pockets of tanzanite are discovered on an average of every two years. At that time the market is flooded with gems, and the price usually drops dramatically. When the pocket is worked out, the price rises again.

Far more rare and more valuable is tsavorite, a local stone found only in Tanzania and neighboring Kenya. Tsavorite is a rich green, the color of the finest emerald. Tsavorite is found in small "pockets" that have to be carefully excavated. After the area has been surveyed by a geologist, the miner begins to work the claim, removing earth until he locates the pocket. Then the stones are

A "pocket" of tsavorite (above); cut and polished tanzanite (inset)

dug out by hand, using simple tools. There are many small gemstone mines located along the Umba River. Tanzania also has become an important source of fine gem rubies.

OTHER MINING

In addition to gemstone mining, many Tanzanians search for gold, found in the northwest near Lake Victoria. There are an untold number of individual gold miners in the region. Because these are illegal operations, without government permits or licenses, the miners usually work at night.

Not all gold mining in Tanzania is illegal. A gold mine owned by the State Mining Corporation was established with aid from Finland. This mine had a short life span—only about fifteen years. There are other gold mines in Tanzania, including the Buckreef mine in Geita, south of Lake Victoria.

Young boys walk carrying large bundles of beans (above).
A few people are able to afford a bicycle (inset).

TRANSPORTATION

Transportation facilities are limited to a few specific areas and needs. Few people travel just for pleasure or to get to work, like people in most Western countries. There is very little private car ownership. The principal means of transport is the bicycle, though not many people can afford one. The people riding bicycles are almost always men. They use them to go to and from work. The railroads, boat transport, and the roads are nearly all directed toward the needs of business and the economy. People who want to visit their families often use river and lake transport. On Lake Victoria, ferries take people to the ports of Mwanza, Bukoba, and Musoma on Tanzania's side of the lake, as well as to ports in Kenya and Uganda. People walk great distances along the roads. The railroad is too expensive for most people because there are so few wage-earning jobs.

The Chinese supplied funds and labor to help build the Tazara rail line in the 1970s.

At the time of independence Tanzania had a rail network to transport agricultural products. The northern line, running from the port of Tanga, crossed to the sisal-producing areas and then to the coffee-growing regions around Mount Kilimanjaro and Mount Meru. The second line ran from Dar es Salaam to the town of Kigoma on Lake Tanganyika; a branch line connected to Mwanza, on Lake Victoria, where cotton was grown.

Construction of a new rail line, the Tazara, was begun in 1970, to run from Dar es Salaam to the Zambian border. It went into service in 1975, thanks to funds and labor supplied by the Chinese. The line was a remarkable achievement, built to run through very difficult terrain, including mountains, swampland, and the Selous Game Reserve. Although the original Chinese locomotives had to be replaced by German-made engines, and in

Dhows at anchor in the Indian Ocean

spite of maintenance problems, the train continues to carry passengers from the port of Dar es Salaam through southern Tanzania to the town of Kapiri Mposhi in Zambia, several hundred miles south of the Tanzanian border.

DHOWS

Along the Indian Ocean coast, dhows carry people and goods from port to port and island to island. These distinctive sailboats, which originated in India but are now built locally on the Kenyan and Tanzanian coast and islands, depend on the wind for their motion. Men still go out in fishing dhows from Zanzibar and the other offshore islands, fishing the warm ocean waters. Although more modern and larger boats are now in use as passenger ferries, dhows continue to be used for freight and for deep-sea fishing.

Dhows traveled regularly from Arabia and the Persian Gulf in the north to Zanzibar. They were able to make the trip to the

The busy harbor at Dar es Salaam

south and then return north because the strong monsoon winds shift during the year. When the winds blew from the southeast, from April to October, dhows traveled north. When the wind shifted, from November to March, they could travel south. Ocean currents changed along these patterns as well. People had to plan very carefully, timing their travels according to the wind. A few dhows still make the trip between Zanzibar and the Persian Gulf.

STAMPS

Postage stamps can tell a lot about a country. For Tanzania, issuing postage stamps has become a good business. Tanzania issues more stamps each year than all but three other countries, about three hundred different designs a year. The stamps are on all kinds of subjects, including a series of nine Elvis Presley stamps that came out about a year before the United States version.

In Swahili Dar es Salaam *means "haven of peace."*

Dar es Salaam's city market

Chapter 8

THE CITIES

DAR ES SALAAM

Dar es Salaam has been an important port city on the East African coast for more than one hundred years. Its name means "haven of peace" in Swahili. Its deep natural harbor was its main attraction in 1866, when the sultan of Zanzibar planned to create a port and trading center here. In 1887 the Germans took over the territory and turned the sultan's plan into reality. They created much of the present look of the official buildings in Dar, as the city is called. Missionaries soon followed, building their distinctive churches.

From these beginnings, a major city grew; today, it is estimated that almost 1.5 million people live here. The nation's two major

Some views of Dar es Salaam: the main railroad station (above),
shoppers in the city market (below left), and a traffic
policewoman talking to a motorbike driver (below right)

The Askari Monument in downtown Dar es Salaam honors the Africans who fought and died in World War I. Askari *means "soldier" in Swahili.*

railroads both end up in Dar, bringing goods to the port. For visitors to Dar the markets around India Street are always a delight. Here, the goods offered by Asian traders give the area an Oriental look. The National Museum displays some of the archaeological finds made at Olduvai Gorge.

DODOMA

Dodoma is located in the exact geographic center of the country, 300 miles (483 kilometers) west of Dar es Salaam. Once just a collection of huts, Dodoma became an important railroad stop in 1910. Although there was little to justify development—water was in very short supply—Dodoma's location continued to attract attention, and it slowly grew into a real city. In 1973 President Nyerere declared that Dodoma would become Tanzania's capital. Although nearly $1 billion was spent in the process, the official government remains in Dar es Salaam.

Arusha (above) is the safari center of Tanzania and the place where meerschaum pipes (inset) are made.

ARUSHA

Located close to Mount Meru, Arusha is a pretty town that serves as the safari center of Tanzania. Kilimanjaro International Airport allows visitors to fly directly into Arusha. From here, tourists can easily reach many of the country's best-known wildlife reserves, including Serengeti, Ngorongoro Crater, and Olduvai Gorge. Arusha is also the center of the country's meerschaum carvers. Meerschaum is a soft, white mineral that is carved into elaborate smokers' pipes. The largest deposit of this mineral in the world is found in Tanzania, near Lake Amboseli. Arusha's many craft shops also sell Makonde sculptures, the elegant pieces made from ebony.

Mwanza (above) is on the shore of Lake Victoria.
Mount Meru (inset) is just north of Arusha.

MWANZA

Mwanza, on the southern shore of Lake Victoria, is an important port as well as the last stop on the rail line from Tabora. Its position on the lake makes it a center for commerce as well as fishing. The Sukuma people live in this region. Their traditional culture may be studied at the Bujora Sukuma Village Museum, about ten miles (sixteen kilometers) from the town.

TANGA

The port of Tanga is Tanzania's fourth-largest city. Its northerly position on the coast puts it directly across the water from the island of Pemba, which is administered by Zanzibar. Not far from Tanga are some ancient burial sites and limestone caves.

The Ngorongoro Crater is like a natural zoo with animals such as zebras (above) and elephants (below) roaming freely in it.

Chapter 9

THE NATURAL ENVIRONMENT

THE LAST PLACE ON EARTH

Tanzania is one of the last places where it is possible to take a look back in history, not through the pages of a book but through nature itself. Because so little of the land has been developed and changed by people, researchers of all kinds see Tanzania as a huge, open-air classroom. The game parks, where development is restricted or forbidden, are living laboratories where nature can be studied and recorded, with some studies taking place over several decades.

Every year millions of wildebeests, with some zebras mixed in, make their way across Tanzania's plains in a spectacle that reminds us of what the earth may have looked like before human beings took over so much of the land.

Tanzania itself has been the backdrop for a number of adventure films, especially in the 1950s. Among the best known are *Mogambo* with Clark Gable, Grace Kelly, and Ava Gardner; *Stanley and Livingstone* with Spencer Tracy; and *Tanganyika* with Van Heflin.

A giraffe in the Serengeti National Park

SERENGETI

The Serengeti National Park came to the world's attention with the publication of Dr. Bernard Grzimek's book, *Serengeti Shall Not Die*. The title was really a plea for help, for Dr. Grzimek saw how easily the Serengeti could be lost if there were no controls over its use. There is pressure for farmland from the constantly growing human population. The local people see the drawbacks, not the benefits, of the wildlife. The animals invade farms and eat crops; they sometimes attack and kill domestic animals.

The plains of the Serengeti are fertile, although the land itself is quite fragile. In 1937 the Serengeti was set aside as a game reserve, and it became a national park in 1951. Thanks to the research and energies of Dr. Grzimek, its boundaries were expanded to approximately the size it is today. Grzimek showed that if the animals were too restricted in their movements during migrations, their whole population was threatened.

The Serengeti National Park is part of a vast region known as the Serengeti Ecosystem, covering 10,000 square miles (25,900 square kilometers). It includes areas where only wildlife are allowed and areas where wildlife and people, usually the Maasai with their livestock, use the same land. Within the ecosystem are both Serengeti National Park and the Ngorongoro Conservation Area. Serengeti National Park alone covers 5,700 square miles (14,763 square kilometers)–the size of the state of Connecticut. The Maasai called it *siringet*, meaning "endless plains" or "endless expanse."

THE MIGRATION

What makes the Serengeti unique is the migration of the wildebeests (also known as gnu). The year-round cycle begins in the south, where the wildebeests gather on the open plains to feed on the new grass that grows after the rains. Natural instincts determine every aspect of the migration. The wildebeests are about to give birth, and the new grass provides extra calcium for their milk.

As many as two million animals gather every year. The greatest mass of animals may be seen in January and February. By the end of February, within the space of one month, virtually all of the calves have been born. A wildebeest calf is on its feet within minutes and can run at full speed in less than fifteen minutes. It has to if it expects to survive–the herds are accompanied by lions, hyenas, leopards, and other predators. They look for the easiest prey, which is often a newborn calf.

Wildebeests in Ngorongoro Crater (above) and crossing
a river during migration (inset)

The animals are always on the move, but their movement
increases dramatically by May as they head north through the
Serengeti and across the Kenyan border. As they cross the Mara
River, many animals, sometimes tens of thousands, are lost in the
rapid current. But one to two million survivors arrive to spend
July and August grazing in the Maasai Mara, located in Kenya in
a northern extension of the Serengeti. As the grass is used up, the
animals begin to move southward again, returning to the
Serengeti by November for the next rainy season.

OTHER WILDLIFE

Many other animals live in the Serengeti, including Maasai
giraffes, a species marked by ragged-edged splotches of brown

Ostriches (left), impalas (top), and golden weaver birds (right) live in the Serengeti.

against its tan hide. There are fierce Cape buffalo, elephants, lions, great herds of zebras, ostriches, and many kinds of antelope, including gazelles, impalas, eland, and topis.

Bird life is varied and colorful, highlighted by the superb starlings, lilac-breasted rollers, crested cranes, and the many weaver birds. Weaver birds build amazing nests, deftly weaving grasses together with their beaks. They build the nests far out on the thinnest branches of the trees to keep the nests out of reach of predators.

Above: In Ngorongoro Crater wildebeests and zebras graze while vultures circle overhead. Flamingos feed on Lake Magadi in the background. Inset: A saddlebill stork

At the Serengeti Research Institute, teams of ecologists and students of animal behavior have conducted long-term research projects that use the whole Serengeti Ecosystem as the basis for their fieldwork. Among the best known is Dr. George Schaller's study of lions.

NGORONGORO CRATER

Within the Serengeti Ecosystem, east of the park, lies Ngorongoro Crater. The name *Ngorongoro* is taken from a Maasai word that refers to the sound of the bells the Maasai wore into battle. When the people heard the Maasai warriors' bells, they were terrified, which is probably why some people think the word means "a cold place."

This vast crater resulted from a volcanic eruption millions of years ago. The lava dome that was created collapsed and formed a perfect crater, or "caldera," which is the correct term for this formation. The caldera is 11 miles (17.7 kilometers) across, with nearly straight walls. The floor of the crater is like a natural zoo, where animals live out their whole life cycle. The caldera floor with its swamps and forests lies nearly 2,000 feet (610 meters) below the rim.

About twenty-five thousand creatures—birds and beasts—live within the caldera. Flamingos come to Lake Magadi, a salty soda lake, to feed. Changing levels of water in the lake, and the shift from dry to rainy seasons, lead to the arrival and departure of many species of birds, including the blacksmith plover, saddlebill stork, ibis, and others. Migrating birds come from thousands of miles away to escape the winter season in Europe.

LAKE NATRON

Many bird species live in Tanzania for only part of the year or for a breeding season. This is true of the beautiful flamingos, those graceful pink birds with the pencil-thin legs. For much of the year, the flamingos mass around Lake Nakuru, in Kenya, although they might turn up elsewhere one year and then return to Nakuru the next.

When the flamingos are ready to breed, they always return to Lake Natron, in the north of Tanzania, near the mountain called

Jane Goodall (above) in 1989 with one of her beloved chimpanzees, and flamingos (right) on Lake Natron

Ol Doinyo Lengai, the Maasai name for "mountain of god." Lengai is an active volcano that last erupted in 1966. Lake Natron provides the flamingos with the breeding conditions they like. They build their nests out on the soda flats that float in the lake, whose water is strongly corrosive because of the large amount of alkaline salts it contains. This helps protect them from predators. The flamingos are the only large animals that can live in these conditions.

GOMBE STREAM

Gombe Stream is a tiny wildlife reserve, now set aside as a national park. Tucked away in a corner of Tanzania, on the shore of Lake Tanganyika, it measures just 10 miles (16 kilometers) long by 3 miles (4.8 kilometers) wide and is very mountainous. In the forests of this small preserve live families of chimpanzees who are free to roam. They have been followed very closely over a long period of time by Jane Goodall. Her research established many facts about the life of chimpanzees that were not known before. She found that they use tools to get at food, that they like to eat meat, and that they are highly organized in their social behavior. She spent so much time working here that the chimps became used to having people around them. This has made it possible for tourists to visit the park and see the chimps. Jane Goodall proved that one dedicated person could take on a subject no one had ever followed and add to the knowledge of natural history.

OLDUVAI GORGE

To the casual visitor, Olduvai Gorge is a dry, desolate place. Though located within the Serengeti, in the Ngorongoro Conservation Area, this is not a place to view animals. But within this gorge, only twenty-five miles (forty kilometers) long, Mary and Louis Leakey made some of the most important discoveries regarding the origins of mankind. There Mary Leakey discovered one of man's ancestors, the two-million-year-old *Australopithecus boisei*, and changed our theories about how long human life has existed on earth. The very dryness of Olduvai proved to be vital in preserving the traces of early man. Starting from about ten thousand years ago, two million years of life, in layers, could be traced back. The work began in 1931, but the first important find was made in 1959. The Leakeys showed that man descended from several branches, not from a direct line back to a common ancestor.

Very recently, footprints were found in the gorge that are believed to have been made four million years ago. Two people

Olduvai Gorge (above) is where Mary and Louis Leakey made their discoveries. The Leakeys (inset) display the upper jaw and skull that they found in 1959. Dr. Leakey estimated these finds to be six hundred thousand years old.

walked across ash left on the plain; then a light rain fell and filled in the prints; finally, the prints dried and hardened. And then they were left untouched for four million years.

A re-creation at the American Museum of Natural History in New York City shows what these people might have looked like as they walked across Tanzania.

SELOUS GAME RESERVE

Selous Game Reserve is the largest in all of Africa, yet it is also one of the least-known wildlife regions. It was named for Frederick Selous, a hunter who guided President Theodore

An adult and baby elephant foraging for food

Roosevelt when he went on safari in Africa. The Selous is riddled
with rivers and an absorbent kind of soil that can turn to swamp
underfoot. Although first set aside as a small game reserve in
1905, its current boundaries were set by a determined park
warden, C.J.P. Ionides, in the 1930s. There was not much
competition for the land because it is almost impossible for people
to live here. In the rainy season the reserve's many rivers
overflow and spill out onto the floodplains, sweeping everything
aside. In most areas of the reserve there are no roads; the park is
infested with tsetse flies, and thick miombo forests cover the land.
In the dry season the land turns hard and huge cracks appear,
guaranteeing that vehicles will not get through.

As a result, the reserve is well suited to its only purpose: to
protect the wildlife and allow it to prosper. Here are found huge
numbers of elephants, hippopotamuses, kudu, crocodiles, and
hundreds of species of birds. Only a tiny portion of the reserve is

visited by tourists, some of them arriving on the Tazara railroad that cuts across the northwest part of Selous. Some enjoy boat rides on the Rufiji River, one of the best ways to get around this swampy region. The animals are much less used to tourists and so they act differently, more like their true selves. Unlike Ngorongoro Crater, where the lions will not move even when a vehicle drives right up to them, the Selous offers a truer experience of being in the wilderness. A new national park has been established in the Uzungwa Mountains, just west of Selous. This rain-forest region has many species of plant life that have never been identified.

CLIMBING KILIMANJARO

Although Kilimanjaro is the highest mountain in Africa, its shape makes it a uniquely accessible mountain for climbing. Kilimanjaro can be climbed by almost anyone who is fit. Tens of thousands of people climb it every year. It dominates the landscape and the image of Tanzania around the world. People did not believe the early explorers' reports of a snowcapped mountain nearly on the equator. Kilimanjaro has three peaks, but climbers usually aim for Uhuru Point on Kibo Peak, at the very top of the 19,340-foot (5,895-meter) mountain. *Uhuru* means "freedom" in Swahili.

MWEKA WILDLIFE COLLEGE

The College of African Wildlife Management at Mweka, near Mount Kilimanjaro, is a unique school where people learn how to manage wildlife. Tanzanians, as well as foreigners, come to this facility that was established more than thirty years ago. Patrick Hemingway, son of Ernest Hemingway, was a teacher here for many years, teaching people how to maintain and manage the wildlife. Many wildlife conservation groups, including the World Wildlife Fund, contribute to the school.

TOURISTS RETURN

The years of devotion to socialism and the closing of the border with Kenya took their toll on Tanzania's tourism. But with the reopening of the border in 1983, the country began to look once again to tourism as a way of bringing in money. The natural environment–the wildlife and the geography–are unequaled anywhere in Africa, but the facilities were in almost total disrepair. Slowly, though, things are improving.

ZANZIBAR

Zanzibar is a unique tourist destination. Visitors don't come here for wildlife; they come to see history. The rich Swahili culture, a combination of Asian, Arab, and African influences, can be found on every street. The unique smells of spicy cooking and the sight of artisans restoring historic buildings are part of this quiet kind of tourism.

Zanzibar is famous for its carved doors. Virtually every house has a handsome wooden door with individual carvings of fruits and flowers and quotations from the Koran, the Muslim holy book. The quotations are meant to protect the inhabitants of the house. The doors are so valued that they have been counted; there are more than 560 of them, some of them dating back to the end

Scenes of Zanzibar: an old Arab fort (top left);
the house where David Livingstone stayed in 1866, now
used as the tourist office (top right); wooden carved
doors in Arabic style (left); and loading passengers
onto a hydrofoil that links Zanzibar to the
mainland (above)

of the seventeenth century. The feeling of the old sultanate can still be felt on the streets of Zanzibar, the same flavor that survives in neighboring Lamu and Mombasa in Kenya.

There are ancient ruins on the island that have survived through the centuries because they were built of stone, often of the same coral that forms the island itself. A historic restoration commission, funded by the Norwegians, is now overseeing repairs on many of the old buildings.

Zanzibar is known as the departure point for the nineteenth-century explorers. Tourists can stop off at Livingstone House to see where the adventurers gathered their supplies. Livingstone House was home for Dr. Livingstone while he got ready for his last expedition; Stanley used it later as he prepared to cross the mainland.

The undersea life off the coast of Zanzibar and Pemba offers its own kind of sightseeing. Visitors can go snorkeling or diving among the coral reefs and see the tropical fish. Although fishing was very good in this region, it has been hurt by the fishermen's practice of exploding dynamite in the water to bring the fish to the surface. This is destroying the coral reef.

To reach Zanzibar from the mainland, there are several choices. The fastest is the hydrofoil, a boat that rides on a retractable fin that lifts the hull clear of the water as speed increases. There are also catamarans and passenger ferries. Air Zanzibar has connections from the mainland. The Zanzibaris want to limit the number of mainlanders who settle on the island. With its small land area and population of 700,000, Zanzibar just cannot afford to accept everyone who wants to come here to try to make a living.

A hotel under construction in Dar es Salaam (above) and President Ali Hassan Mwinyi (left)

Chapter 10

MODERN TANZANIA

When former President Nyerere gave up the chairmanship of the political party in 1990, he released his last hold on power in Tanzania. This allowed President Ali Hassan Mwinyi to get the country moving ahead.

Through all the years since independence, Tanzania has been a one-party nation. Because of this anyone who wanted to hold a political position such as president had to belong to the only political party allowed. Anyone who disagreed with the ideas of that party had no way to offer the people an alternative. Now, under pressure from nations and agencies that pay for many of Tanzania's projects, the government has decided to allow democratic reform and permit other political parties.

Opening up the political process to a more democratic system has been taking place in other African nations, and Tanzania has been watching closely to see how they manage to make the transition. Recently, Tanzanians saw how Kenya handled its first multiparty elections, held on December 29, 1992. Tanzanians noted that the opposition parties, those who wanted to elect a different president, were very disorganized. They were fighting among themselves, instead of uniting into a strong opposition. As a result, the same president, Daniel arap Moi, was able to remain in power. Tanzanian political figures learned a great deal from Kenya's election and hope to do better when they hold their first multiparty elections in 1995.

Tanzanians have an advantage over many other African cultures. Because the government put so much emphasis on teaching everyone to read and write, the country has one of the highest literacy rates in Africa. Now the people will be able to read about the candidates and make their own decisions.

Although former President Nyerere was right in his belief that people should be self-reliant, today Tanzania remains dependent on foreign aid. Whenever a major project is considered, such as building or repairing a road, the Tanzanian government looks for a foreign donor for the money, and often for foreign experts to do the work. As a result, the local people don't gain the skills and knowledge to do the work for themselves.

RELATIONS WITH OTHER COUNTRIES

Tanzania's relationship with Kenya has improved since the border between the countries was reopened. It is once again possible for tourists to take an overland route all the way from Kenya through Tanzania and eventually to Johannesburg in South Africa. They travel along the TanZam road, built in the 1970s.

The end of the long war in Mozambique has made the southern part of Tanzania more secure as well. Many refugees escaped over that border during the war, and Tanzania was known as a generous host to them. Over the next years, they will be assisted in returning to their home country. With most of the countries in

*Left: Former President Julius Nyerere (seated on left) attends
a meeting of the Frontline States in 1985. Right: Salim Salim,
head of the Organization of African Unity*

the region becoming stabilized, Tanzania has been able to turn its
attention to its internal problems.

The Organization of African Unity (OAU), which functions as a
kind of United Nations of Africa, is now headed by a Tanzanian,
Salim Salim, who is from Zanzibar. He was Tanzania's
ambassador to the United Nations from 1970 to 1980 and prime
minister of Tanzania from 1984 to 1985. As head of the OAU since
1989, he represents Tanzania at the highest level.

During the struggle to end the white-minority rule in South
Africa, members of South Africa's leading opposition to apartheid,
the ANC, were given refuge in Tanzania. From 1976, in addition
to being president of Tanzania, Nyerere was the chairman of the
Frontline States, a name given to the nations in southern Africa
that joined together to fight against South Africa's policy of
apartheid. With the April 27, 1994 election in South Africa, where
voting was open to people of all races, Tanzania gained a
powerful new ally in place of its former foe.

MAP KEY

Arusha	B6	Kisaki	C6	Natron, Lake	B6
Arusha (province)	B5, B6, C6	Kisiju	C6	Ndala	B5
Babati	B6	Kisiwani	B6	Newala	D6
Bagamoyo	C6	Kitangari	D6	Ngara	B5
Bereku	B6	Kondoa	B6	Njombe	C5
Bugene	B5	Korogwe	C6	Nyamtumbo	D6
Bukene	B5	Kwa Mtoro	C6	Nyasa, Lake	C5, D5, D6
Bukoba	B5	Lindi	C6	Nzega	B5
Chake Chake	C6	Liwale	C6	Oldeani	B6
Chamba	D6	Loliondo	B6	Pangani	C6
Chunya	C5	Lushoto	B6	Pemba (island)	B6, C6
Coast (province)	C6	Madaba	C6	Pemba (province)	B6, C6
Dar es Salaam	C6	Mafia (island)	C6	Rufiji (river)	C6
Dodoma (province)	B6, C6	Mahenge	C6	Rukwa, Lake	C5
Dodoma	C6	Mahuta	D6	Rungwa	C5
Eyasi, Lake	B5, D6	Manda	D5	Ruvu	C6
Geita	B5	Manyara, Lake	B6	Ruvuma (province)	C6, D5, D6
Great Ruaha (river)	C5, C6	Manyoni	C5	Ruvuma (river)	D6, D7
Handeni	C6	Mara (province)	B5, B6	Sadani	C6
Ifakara	C6	Masai Steppe	B6, C6	Same	B6
Inyonga	C5	Masasi	D6	Sao Hill	C6
Iringa	C6	Mbamba Bay	D5	Sekenke	B5
Iringa (province)	C5, C6, D5, D6	Mbeya (province)	C5	Serengeti Plain	B5, B6
Issuna	C5	Mbeya	C5	Shanwa	B5
Itigi	C5	Mchinga	C6	Shinyanga	B5
Kagera (river)	B5	Mdandu	C5	Shinyanga (province)	B5, B6
Kahama	B5	Meru, Mt. (peak)	B6	Singida	B5
Kalambo Falls	C5	Mikindani	D7	Singida (province)	B5, B6, C5, C6
Kaliua	C5	Mikumi	C6	Songea	D6
Karema	C5	Mingoyo	D6	Sumbawanga	C5
Kasanga	C5	Mkalama	B5	Tabora	C5
Kasulu	B5	Mnyusi	C6	Tanga	C6
Kibau	C6	Mohoro	C6	Tanga (province)	B6, C6
Kiberege	C6	Morogoro	C6	Tanganyika, Lake	B4, C4, C5
Kibondo	B5	Morogoro (province)	C6	Tobora (province)	B5, C5
Kidugallo	C6	Moshi	B6	Tukuyu	C5
Kigoma (province)	B4, B5, C4, C5	Mpanda	C5	Tunduru	D6
Kigoma	B4	Mpwapwa	C6	Tutubu	C5
Kilimanjaro (province)	B6	Mtakuja	C5	Ugalla (river)	C5
Kilimanjaro (peak)	B6	Mtwara	D7	Ujiji	B4
Kilimatinde	C5	Mtwara (province)	D6, D7	Ukerewe (island)	B5
Kilindoni	C6	Muhutwe	B5	Utete	C6
Kilosa	C6	Musoma	B5	Uvinza	C5
Kilwa Kisiwani	C6	Mwadui	B5	Victoria, Lake	A5, B5
Kilwa Kivinje	C6	Mwanza (province)	B5	Wami (river)	C6
Kimamba	C6	Mwanza	B5	Wembere (river)	B5, C5
Kintinku	C6	Mwaya	C5	West Lake (province)	B5
Kinyangiri	B5	Nachingwea	D6	Wete	C6
Kipembawe	C5	Namanyere	C5	Zanzibar (island)	C6
Kipili	C5	Nansio	B5	Zanzibar	C6

112

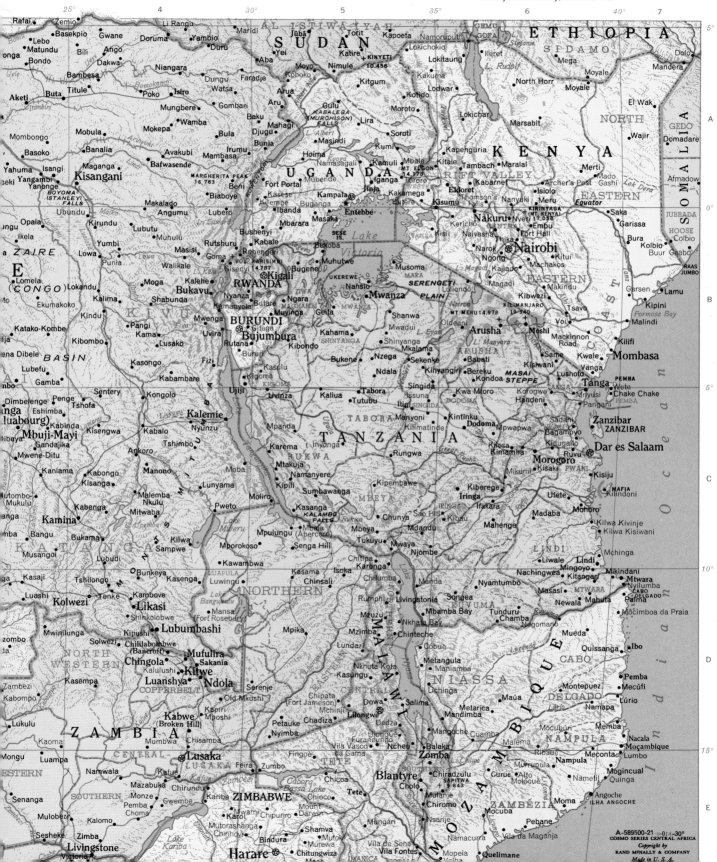

MINI FACTS AT A GLANCE

GENERAL INFORMATION

Official Name: United Republic of Tanzania, *Jamhuri ya Muungano wa Tanzania* in Swahili

Capital: Dar es Salaam (The capital is in the process of being shifted to Dodoma; the legislative branch meets in Dodoma.)

Government: Tanzania is a republic with one legislative house, National Assembly, of 244 members. At present there is only one political party, but a multi-party system was approved in a 1992 vote; the current one-party parliament will stay in force until the next election in 1995. Executive power lies with the president, popularly elected for a five-year period. The president's term is limited to a maximum of two five-year periods. The president appoints two vice-presidents, one of whom is the president of Zanzibar and the other prime minister of the union. The highest court is the Tanzania Court of Appeals. For administrative purposes the country is divided into 25 regions, of which 20 are on the mainland, three on Zanzibar Island, and two on Pemba Island.

Administrative power is shared by both Zanzibar Island and the Tanzania mainland. If the president is from the mainland, the vice-president must be from Zanzibar, or the other way around. Ten members represent Zanzibar in the National Assembly.

Religion: Tanzania does not support any official religion. Some 34 percent of the population is Christian and 33 percent is Muslim. Some people follow the traditional beliefs, and other religions make up the rest of the population. Some Tanzanian Christians continue to practice traditional religions along with their Christian beliefs. Almost all the people of Zanzibar are Muslims.

Ethnic Composition: Nearly 95 percent of the people are black Africans of Bantu origin. Sukuma is the single largest ethnic group making up some 13 percent of the total population; other major groups are Maasai, Nyamwezi, Hehe, Bena, Makonde, Chaga, and Haya. San (Bushmen) and Khoikhoi (Hottentot) are the earliest hunter-gatherer people in Africa. Shirazi, who believe they are descendants of early Persian (Iranian) Muslim settlers who intermarried with local African people, live in Zanzibar. There is a large Indian community basically involved in running small businesses.

Language: Both English and Swahili are national languages. A Bantu language, Swahili has vocabulary from Arabic, Persian, English, German, and Hindi. Most of the native people speak at least one other ethnic language along with Swahili. English is widely used in business, higher education, and government.

National Flag: The present flag was adopted in 1964 at the unification of Zanzibar and Tanzania. The flag has a broad black stripe running diagonally from the left bottom corner to the upper fly. Two narrow yellow-gold stripes run parallel to the black stripe on each side, representing the country's mineral resources. The rest of the flag is green (representing the fertile land) above the black stripe and blue (representing the Indian Ocean) below it.

National Emblem: A native shield is divided into four horizontal parts and is flanked by a barefoot youth and a girl standing on a mound representing Mount Kilimanjaro. The national motto in Swahili, *Uhuru na Umoja*, "Freedom and Unity," appears on a white ribbon in red-gold letters. The emblem has several symbols on the shield, such as an ax and hoe (tools of development), a spear (defense), a flaming torch (freedom and knowledge), and cotton and cloves (leading agricultural resources).

National Anthem: *"Mungu Ibariki Afrika"* ("God the Almighty Bless Africa")

National Calendar: Gregorian

Money: The Tanzania shilling (T sh) consists of 100 cents. In 1995 one Tanzania shilling was worth approximately $0.004 in United States currency.

Membership in International Organizations: African Development Bank (ADB); Frontline States; Non-aligned Movement; Organization of African Unity (OAU); United Nations (UN)

Weights and Measures: The metric system is in use.

Population: 30,742,000 (1995 estimates); 84 persons per sq. mi. (32 persons per sq km); 76 percent rural and 24 percent urban.

Cities:

Dar es Salaam	1,360,850
Mwanza	223,013
Dodoma	203,833
Tanga	187,634
Zanzibar	157,634

(Population figures based on 1988 census.)

GEOGRAPHY

Border: Tanzania is bordered by the Indian Ocean to the east, Kenya to the north, Uganda, Lake Victoria, Rwanda, and Burundi to the northwest, Zaire (Lake Tanganyika) to the west, and Malawi (Lake Malawi), Mozambique, and Zambia to the south.

Coastline: The Indian Ocean coastline is 500 mi. (805 km) long.

Land: Tanzania is located just south of the equator on the east coast of Africa. A great rift valley runs through the center. The Maasai Steppe (grasslands) form most of the central part of the country. The coastal area is low and narrow. The mountain system extends from north to southwest. The Pare and Usambara ranges are near the northeast coast. The highland culminates in Mount Kilimanjaro in the north, just south of the equator. Once an active volcano, it is always topped with snow. Zanzibar Island is separated from the mainland by a 22 mi. (35 km) channel. Zanzibar and Pemba islands are made entirely of a coral substance. There are several very small islands off the coast.

Highest Point: Mount Kilimanjaro, 19,340 ft. (5,895 m); also the highest mountain in Africa

Lowest Point: Lake Tanganyika, 2,289 ft. (698 m) below sea level; also the lowest point in Africa

Rivers: An extensive system of rivers crisscross the country. Major rivers are the Ruvuma, separating Tanzania from Mozambique in the south; the Rufiji; the Wami; and the Pangani. There are many smaller seasonal rivers.

Lakes: Lake Victoria, shared by Uganda and Tanzania, is the largest lake in Africa with 26,828 sq. mi. (69,484 sq km) surface area; it is the third largest in the world after the Caspian Sea and Lake Superior. This freshwater lake is home to the Nile perch and tilapia. Lake Tanganyika is the longest (419 mi.; 674 km) freshwater lake in the world; it is also extremely deep. Lake Nyasa, another narrow and deep lake, has about two hundred different species of fish.

Forests: Some 46 percent of the land is under forests, and another 40 percent is under meadows and pastures. Wooded grasslands cover large areas throughout the country. Coastal areas have mangrove forests. Ebony wood is used by the Makonde people to sculpt "family tree" statues. The *nyinga* wood is prized by musicians throughout the world for making clarinets.

Wildlife: Tanzania has a wide variety of wildlife. Millions of animals of some 430 species and subspecies roam in the wild. Wildlife includes Maasai giraffes, cape buffalo, elephants, lions, rhinoceroses, zebras, hippopotamuses, kudu, crocodiles, ostriches, gazelles, impalas, eland, and topi. A variety of monkeys is found throughout the country. Bird life is superb and colorful including rollers, flamingos, blacksmith plover, saddlebill storks, ibis, cranes, and many weaver birds.

Some of the best-known wildlife reserves are Serengeti, Ngorongoro Crater, Gombe Stream, Selous Game Reserve, and Olduvai Gorge. Hunting is banned or restricted in most of the game reserves. The Serengeti National Park covers a 5,700 sq. mi. (14,763 sq km) area. The annual migration of the wildebeests (gnu) is unique to the Serengeti. Families of chimpanzees roam free in Gombe Stream National Park. The Selous Game Reserve has some 50,000 elephants—one of the largest elephant populations of Africa. The 11 mi. (17.7 km) wide caldera of Ngorongoro Crater is like a natural zoo, where about 25,000 creatures live. Arusha is the safari center of Tanzania.

Climate: Located close to the equator, temperatures change very little in Tanzania throughout the year. Year-round temperatures average about 90° F. (32° C) on the coast. The rainy season lasts for several months—from March through June in the north and from October through March in the south. Near Lake Nyasa there may be more than 100 in. (254 cm) of rain a year, while in the central plateau less than 20 in. (51 cm) falls in a year. The coastal plains are hot and humid, the central plateau is arid and dry, the lake regions are humid and cooler, and the highland areas have a temperate climate.

Greatest Distance: North to South: 760 mi. (1,223 km)
East to West: 740 mi. (1,191 km)

Area: 364,900 sq. mi. (945,087 sq km); includes about 22,800 sq. mi. (59,052 sq km) area under lakes.

ECONOMY AND INDUSTRY

Agriculture: Less than 6 percent of the area is under permanent cultivation. Almost 90 percent of the land is worked in small plots with very simple tools. A number of food and cash crops are grown in Tanzania. Cassava, corn, sugarcane, bananas, plantains, rice, sorghum, coconuts, sweet potatoes, beans, millet, mangoes, peanuts, and potatoes are the chief crops. Cotton, coffee, tobacco, and cashew nuts are the chief cash crops. Rice, sugarcane, and wheat are grown on large plantations. Coffee is grown on small farms at the higher elevations. Cloves, an aromatic spice, have been grown on Zanzibar for many years. Sisal growing was once very important, but it has been recently pushed aside by synthetic substitutes. The southern rim of Lake Victoria is one of the richest agricultural regions in the country.

Large areas are infested by tsetse flies that restrict any livestock raising or agricultural activity. Farmers raise chickens, goats, and sheep. The Maasai people raise cattle in the central region.

Fishing: Victoria, Tanganyika, and Nyasa lakes, and the warm waters of the Indian Ocean, provide rich grounds for fishing. Freshwater fish are sardines, Nile perch, and tilapia. Commercial fisheries have been established on the major lakes and oceanfront. Most of the fish is consumed locally, but more than a million tons of prawns are exported annually.

Mining: Tanzania produces small amounts of diamonds, gemstones (rubies), salt, phosphate, coal, gypsum, kaolin, tin, and gold. Tanzanite is a purple-blue clear gem named for the country. Tsavorite is a rich green stone found in extensive pockets. Many small gemstone mines are located along the Umba River. Tanzania's meerschaum deposits are the largest in the world. Recently some petroleum and natural gas deposits have been located on Songo Songo Island, and further drilling is in progress.

Manufacturing: Major manufacturing items are cement, processed foods, hides and skins, soap, fertilizer, iron sheets, rolled steel, cigarettes, pulp and paper, fertilizer, clothing, footwear, tires, batteries, bricks and tiles, and textiles. There are small oil-refining, metalworking, vehicle assembly, fruit-canning, and engineering factories also. Electricity is chiefly derived from hydroelectric power.

Transportation: In 1990 the total length of railroads was about 2,220 mi. (3,573 km). The country has about 51,023 mi. (82,111 km) of roads, out of which only 5 percent are paved. There are 53 airports and landing strips, and 19 airports have scheduled flights. Dar es Salaam is the major international airport; other international airports are at Kilimanjaro (Arusha) and Zanzibar. Air Tanzania is the international airline; Zanzibar Airways provides service to mainland Tanzania, and Kenya and Uganda. Dar es Salaam is also the chief port with a fine harbor. Other ports are Mtwara and Tanga. Ferry service operates between the ports of Mwanza, Bukoba, and Musoma on Lake Victoria. Along the Indian Ocean small sailboats called dhows carry people and goods from port to port and island to island. Hydrofoil service connects Zanzibar with the mainland. Bicycles are the principal means of personal transport.

Communication: Two daily newspapers are published from Dar es Salaam with a total circulation of about 180,000. There is no television broadcasting on the mainland, only on the island of Zanzibar. But television sets and VCRs are relatively common and there is a thriving video rental trade. Radio broadcasts are in both Swahili and English. Tanzania issues more postage stamps than all but three countries in the world; some 300 different designs are issued each year. In the early 1990s there was one radio receiver per 6 persons, one television set per 315 persons, and one telephone per 174 persons.

Trade: The chief imports are machinery, transport equipment, metals, fuels, consumer goods, and construction materials. The major import sources are the United Kingdom, Germany, Japan, Italy, Sweden, the Netherlands, Denmark, the United States, and Yugoslavia. Chief export items are coffee, beans, raw cotton, sisal, tobacco, cloves, and diamonds. The major export destinations are Germany, the United Kingdom, the Netherlands, Singapore, Italy, Japan, Finland, Portugal, the United States, and France.

EVERYDAY LIFE

Health: Major illnesses are malaria, bilharziasis (from water infected with diseased snails), tuberculosis, pneumonia, polio, and sleeping sickness (carried by tsetse flies). More than 10 percent of the people living in and around the cities are thought to be infected with the AIDS virus. Deficient nutrition is also a major problem. Along with the medical doctors, other medical workers such as medical assistants, rural medical aids, and maternal and health aids are trained to serve the rural countryside better. Tanzania's drinking water quality has increased remarkably in the last three decades. The Flying Doctors service has grown into an important medical institution. In the late 1980s there were some 20,000 persons per physician and one hospital bed per 950 persons. Life expectancy at 50 years for males and 55 years for females is low. Infant mortality rate at 105 per 1,000 births is high.

Education: Some 20 percent of the budget is spent on education; villages are encouraged to build their own schools with government assistance. Education at the primary level is free and compulsory. It begins at seven years of age and lasts for seven years. Secondary education begins at age 14 and lasts for a further six years. The medium of instruction is generally Swahili; English is taught as a second language. Other educational facilities include trade schools, technical and business colleges, and an education college. Vocational training is encouraged by the government. Under the adult literacy campaign, millions of adults learn to read, write, and do some arithmetic every year. In the late 1980s the total literacy rate was about 95 percent—one of the highest in Africa.

The University of Dar es Salaam and Sokoine University of Agriculture are the two major institutions of higher learning. The Serengeti Research Institute conducts long-term animal behavior studies. The College of African Wildlife Management at Mweka teaches people how to manage wildlife.

Holidays:

> New Year's Day, January 1
> Zanzibar Revolution Day, January 12
> Chama Cha Mapinduzi (Revolutionary Party) Day, February 5
> Union Day, April 26
> International Worker's Day, May 1
> Farmers' Day, *Saba Saba* (Seven Seven) Day, July 7
> Independence Day, December 9
> Christmas, December 25

Movable religious holidays include Id al-Fitr, Id al-Adha, Maulid an-Nabi, Good Friday, and Easter Sunday.

Culture: Every ethnic group has its own dance and folklore. Sukuma people are well known for performing the *gobogobo* dance and are traditional snake charmers. Makonde people are best known for their ebony sculptures. Craftspeople in Zanzibar make beautiful wooden chests decorated in geometric patterns with metal strips and brass studs. People in Arusha carve elaborate smoker's pipes from the soft white meerschaum mineral. The Maasai people make elaborate leather shields and beadwork. There is much literature in Swahili; President Nyerere, himself, translated several of Shakespeare's plays into Swahili.

The National Museum at Dar es Salaam displays some of the archaeological, historical, geological, and ethnographical finds. The National Central Library is also at Dar es Salaam. The Bujora Sukuma Village Museum at Mwanza has displays of Sukuma traditions.

Society: People of Tanzania come from 120 different ethnic groups. They live mainly in small villages where kinship is the basis for the community. Relationships can be traced through oral history. The "family" refers to parents, children, aunts, uncles, and in-laws. Neighbors work together to cultivate the land and build houses. Traditionally women do more work than men in Tanzania, as in most of Africa. They raise children, pound grain to make flour, and grow and prepare food. Daily they go out in search of firewood and carry it back home; they carry water back home in small buckets. Even young girls carry water home daily. Recent laws overruled customary African and Islamic laws and gave women more rights. The minimum age for marriage for girls was increased to 15 years so they can stay in school a bit longer. The boy's family must pay bride wealth to the girl's family. Ramadan, the ninth month of the Muslim calendar, is the holiest time for the Muslims.

Dress: Traditionally women wear a colorful wraparound garment called a *kanga* and men wear a wrap called a *kikoi*. Muslim men wear a flowing robe of white called a *kanzu*, and pillbox hat called a *kofia*. Muslim women wear a black, hooded dress called a *buibui*. Western-style clothes are popular in cities. Both Maasai men and women wear elaborate beaded jewelry that they make themselves. When Maasai go to the cities, they wear Western clothing and speak English.

Housing: The majority of people live in rural villages with few modern facilities like running water or electricity. Wood and mud provide the basic raw material for most of the rural homes. Village homes tend to be either rectangular with flat roofs, or circular with thatched roofs. A small garden with chickens accompanies most of the rural homes. In cities houses are made of bricks and stone.

Food: The basic food is *ugali*—a stiff porridge made from corn or other grain flour. It can be eaten alone or with stew when available. Corn forms a large proportion of the entire diet. *Ndizi* is a local banana dish. *Pilau* or *biriani* are spicy rice and meat dishes popular in Zanzibar and along the coast. There are very few fresh vegetables in the Tanzanian diet. Most of the ethnic groups do not eat meat except on special occasions. Cow's milk and blood are an important part of the Maasai diet.

Sports and Recreation: Dancing and singing are the two most common recreations. Soccer is the national game. Running and other Olympic sports have become popular.

Social Welfare: There is no official social welfare program in Tanzania, but the Rural Development Division works to improve labor and health conditions in rural areas. Extended families look after their older relatives. Christian missionary organizations operate in urban areas.

IMPORTANT DATES

600-400 B.C.—The area east of Lake Victoria is inhabited by Bantu-speaking peoples (direct descendents of most modern Tanzanians)

A.D. 100—First historical reference to trade between the West and the coast of East Africa

9th Century—Arabs from the Persian Gulf region explore the coastal regions

12th Century—Swahilis have firmly establish trading posts and small settlements on the coast, city-states like Kilwa at the beginning of several centuries of regional power and trading success

1498—Portuguese explorer Vasco da Gama arrives in East Africa

1698—Portuguese are driven out of Zanzibar

1822—Zanzibar and European powers agree to outlaw slavery

1833—Americans sign a treaty with the sultan of Zanzibar

1837—Americans establish the first consulate at Zanzibar; the sultan of Oman rules the territory of Zanzibar, Pemba, and the mainland coast

1857—British explorers Richard Burton and John Speke reach Lake Tanganyika while searching for the source of the Nile

1866—David Livingstone, a missionary explorer, sets out to discover the source of Nile; the sultan of Zanzibar plans to create a port and trading center at Dar es Salaam

1884-85—The Berlin Conference divides land in Africa among European powers

1886—The sultan of Tanganyika is granted the islands of Zanzibar, Pemba, Mafia, Lamu, and the Tanganyika coast

1887—Germans take over the area surrounding Dar es Salaam and construct most of the present-day buildings

1890—The British gain control of Zanzibar and Pemba and make them a British protectorate

1891—The German government takes over rule of the German territory from the German East Africa Company

1905—*Maji Maji* Rebellion by Africans against German rule begins; Selous Game Reserve is established

1907—*Maji Maji* Rebellion ends with Germans still in control

1910—Dodoma becomes a major railroad stop

1914—World War I breaks out in Europe; the British begin a naval blockade of Tanganyika

1915—The German cruiser *Konigsberg* is sunk in the Rufiji River

1916—The British start pushing into German territory around Mount Kilimanjaro

1917—German soldiers are finally pushed out of Tanganyika by the British

1922—The British informal rule ends in Tanganyika; the League of Nations gives the British responsibility for the region as a "mandated territory"

1929—The African Association is created to develop political awareness among the Africans

1931—Anthropological work begins at the Olduvai Gorge

1937—Serengeti is set aside as a game reserve

1939—The African Association and a similar association from Zanzibar merge; the Williamson diamond mine at Mwadui is discovered

1945—The United Nations (UN) is founded

1946—Tanganyika becomes a United Nations trust territory

1948—The African Association becomes the Tanganyika African Association (TAA)

1951—Serengeti becomes a national park

1954—TAA becomes the Tanganyika African National Union (TANU) with Julius Nyerere as its leader; TANU starts demanding self-government

1957—The African Medical and Research Foundation (AMREF), better known as The Flying Doctors, is set up to deal with medical emergencies in rural areas

1958—Britain allows election of "unofficial members" in the Legislative Council

1959—TANU is the winner in elections; in recognition of the Maasai's unique relationship with wildlife, a portion of the Serengeti is returned to the Maasai people; the first important find is made by Mary and Louis Leakey about the two-million-year-old *Australopithecus boisei*

1960—Julius Nyerere emerges as chief minister of the new Council of Ministers

1961—Internal self-government is achieved with Nyerere as prime minister; Tanganyika becomes a fully independent nation; the University of Dar es Salaam is established

1962—Nyerere takes office as president, but resigns to become a teacher to the whole country; Tanganyika becomes a republic headed by a president; toward the end of the year Nyerere wins overwhelmingly and is elected president

1963—Elections are held in Zanzibar; the ruling power of the sultan of Oman is eliminated; the elected government is overturned, and the Afro-Shirazi party takes control of Zanzibar

1964—The country's name is changed from Tanganyika to Tanzania; the islands of Zanzibar and Pemba join with Tanganyika to form the United Republic of Tanganyika; the name is changed to the United Republic of Tanzania; Tanzania Library Service is established

1965—An interim constitution is proclaimed; diplomatic relations with Great Britain are broken over the Rhodesia issue

1966—Production from the Mwadui diamond mine reaches 924,000 carats; the Lengai Volcano erupts; the Tanzanian shilling is introduced as the new currency replacing the East African shilling

1967—Tanzania, Kenya, and Uganda form the East African Community; East African Airways (EAA) is formed; Arusha Declaration describes the *ujamaa* plan of a new kind of socialist political system based on traditional life in an extended family in a village; Tanzanians consolidate into rural *ujamaa* villages

1968—Swahili becomes the sole official language and the medium of instruction in primary schools; diplomatic relations with Great Britain are restored

1969—Nyerere establishes a family planning association to curb the high birth rate; all primary schools are nationalized

1970—Construction of a new railway line begins from Dar es Salaam and the Zambian border; Nyerere is reelected president

1973—Nyerere declares that Dodoma will become Tanzania's new capital city

1975—The New Tanzara Railway line is opened for traffic

1976—Under President Nyerere's *ujamaa* plan, some 70 percent of the population live in villages and only 30 percent in cities; Nyerere becomes president of the Frontline States

1977—East African Airways collapses; Tanzania closes its borders with Kenya; the East African Community collapses; Tanzania's tourism industry starts declining; Edward Sokoine is named prime minister

1978—Uganda's dictator Idi Amin claims a piece of territory in the northwest of Tanzania; Nyerere recaptures the territory and successfully invades Uganda; Amin flees Uganda; Education Act makes primary education compulsory

1980—Nyerere is reelected in national elections; Zanzibar gets a new constitution, under which it elects its own president; all privately owned medical facilities are nationalized

1981—Tanzanian troops are withdrawn from Uganda

1983—The borders with Kenya are reopened

1984—Prime Minister Sokoine is killed in an auto accident; Sokoine University is opened

1985—Tanzanian bishops travel to Kenya to hear Pope John Paul II at the Forty-third Eucharistic Conference; Nyerere steps down from the presidency

1990—Nyerere gives up the chairmanship of the Tanzania Revolutionary party and is succeeded by Mwinyi

1992—A multiparty system is approved; multiparty election date is set for 1995; Rwanda Peace Talks are held at Arusha

1994—Two Tanzanian peacekeepers and civilians are killed when their convoy is attacked by Hutu extremists hunting Rwandan refugees in Tanzania; the Getty Conservation Institute negotiates a three-year plan with Tanzania to preserve the 3.5 million-year-old footprints at Olduvai Gorge that are the oldest known conclusive evidence of human ancestors walking upright

IMPORTANT PEOPLE

Filbert Bayi (1953-   ), internationally known Tanzanian runner; a former world record holder at 1,500 meters

Sir Richard Francis Burton (1821-90), British explorer and Orientalist; wrote *Zanzibar: City, Island and Coast*; with John Speke explored Lake Tanganyika region in 1858

Dr. Jane Goodall (1934-   ), British ethologist best known for her original and exceptionally detailed research on the chimpanzees of Gombe Stream National Park in Tanzania

Dr. Bernard Grzimek, author; made Serengeti internationally known with his book *Serengeti Shall Not Die*

Patrick Hemingway, son of Ernest Hemingway; taught at the College of African Wildlife Management at Mweka for several years

Abeid Karume (1905-72), of Congolese origin; leader of the Afro-Shirazi political party; first president of Zanzibar (1963); first vice-president of Tanzania

Kinjeketile, traditional doctor who believed in the power of spirits; leader of the *Maji Maji* Rebellion against the Germans

Rashidi Kawawa, prime minister, 1961-62

Johann Ludwig Krapf (1810-81), German missionary and traveler; represented British Church Missionary Society; discovered Mount Kilimanjaro in 1848; translated the New Testament into Swahili

Louis Seymour Bazett Leakey (1903-72), British anthropologist; discovered with Mary Leakey fossils of the two-million-year-old *Australopithecus boisei* at Olduvai Gorge

Mary Douglas Leakey (1913-   ), British anthropologist; wife of Louis Leakey; discovered the two-million-year-old *Australopithecus boisei* at Olduvai Gorge

David Livingstone (1813-73), Scottish missionary and explorer; discovered Lake Nyasa (1859); led expedition to discover source of the Nile (1866)

Ali Hassan Mwinyi (1925-   ), president of Zanzibar during 1984-85; leader of the Revolutionary party and president of Tanzania since 1985

Julius Kambarage Nyerere (1922-   ), also known as *Mwalimu*, "the teacher"; first president of Tanzania (1962), stepped down as president in 1985; chairman of the Frontline States

Johannes Rebmann (1820-76), German missionary and traveler; represented British Church Missionary Society; discovered Mount Kilimanjaro in 1848 with Krapf

Sayyid Said bin Ahmad al-Albusaidi (1791-1856), sultan of Oman; with British help he brought the island of Zanzibar under control

Salim Ahmed Salim (1942-   ), from Zanzibar; head of the Organization of African Unity (OAU) since 1989; president of the United Nations General Assembly during 1979-80; Tanzanian ambassador to the United Nations from 1970 to 1980; foreign minister during 1980-84; prime minister of Tanzania from 1984 to 1985

Frederick Courteney Selous (1851-1917), English explorer and elephant hunter; guided American President Theodore Roosevelt on his safari in Africa; Selous Game Reserve is named after him

Edward Moringe Sokoine (1938-84), prime minister from 1977 to 1980 and 1983 to 1984; of Maasai origin; Sokoine University of Agriculture is named after him

John Hanning Speke (1827-64), British explorer; while searching for the source of the Nile, he reached Lake Tanganyika along with Richard Burton in 1857; reached Lake Victoria and named it after the reigning British queen; declared that Lake Victoria was the source of the Nile

Sir Henry Morton Stanley (1841-1904), British journalist and explorer; "found" Dr. Livingstone in 1871; circumnavigated Lake Victoria and confirmed John Speke's theory that Lake Victoria was the source of the Nile

Dr. John T. Williamson, Canadian geologist; discovered the Mwadui diamond mine in 1939

Dr. Michael Wood, British doctor who with two other doctors established the Flying Doctors service in 1957

Compiled by Chandrika Kaul

INDEX

Page numbers that appear in boldface type indicate illustrations

About the Authors

Ettagale Blauer has been writing about Africa for young adult readers for twenty years. She has written three books, published by Farrar, Straus & Giroux Inc., on South Africa, Portugal, and Bangladesh, in collaboration with Jason Lauré. Their Bangladesh book was nominated for the National Book Award.

She has traveled widely in Africa, including a year in South Africa and a three-month-long trip from Morocco to Kenya. She has visited many diamond and gold mines during her research and says she knows the continent "from beneath the ground and up."

Born in New York City, Ms. Blauer was graduated from Hunter College with a degree in creative writing. Ms. Blauer is also well known in the field of jewelry writing and is the author of *Contemporary American Jewelry Design.*

Jason Lauré was born in Chehalis, Washington, and lived in California before joining the United States army and serving in France. He attended Columbia University and worked for *The New York Times.* He traveled to San Francisco and became a photographer during the turbulent 1960s. He recorded those events before setting out on the first of many trips to Africa.

Mr. Lauré covers the political life of that continent and also has made a number of expeditions across the Sahara. He has written about, and photographed in, forty countries in Africa.

In the Enchantment of the World series, Mr. Lauré has written books on Zimbabwe, Bangladesh, Angola, Zambia, Namibia, and Botswana.

Mr. Lauré is married to Marisia Lauré, a translator. Mr. Lauré is based in New York and spends half of each year in Africa.